Non-Verbal Reasoning

For the CEM (Durham University) test

The 11+ Study Book

and Parents' Guide

This book contains two pull-out sections:

A **Benchmark Test** at the front
A **Parents' Guide to 11+ Non-Verbal Reasoning** at the back

Find the figure in each row that is **most unlike** the other figures.

1.

    a   b   c   d   e   (___)

2.

    a   b   c   d   e   (___)

3.

    a   b   c   d   e   (___)

4.

    a   b   c   d   e   (___)

Find which one of the four squares **completes the sequence** on the left.

5.

          a   b   c   d   (_d_)

6.

          a   b   c   d   (___)

7.

          a   b   c   d   (___)

8.

          a   b   c   d   (___)

Work out which option is a **top-down 2D view** of the 3D figure on the left.

9.

          a   b   c   d   (___)

10.

          a   b   c   d   (___)

11.

          a   b   c   d   (___)

12.

          a   b   c   d   (___)

END OF TEST

/12

Find which one of the four figures on the right is a rotation of the figure on the left.

1. **Rotate**  ...

　　a　　(b)　　(c)　　d　　　　　　(C)

2. **Rotate**   ...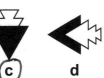

　　a　　b　　(c)　　d　　　　　　(C)

3. **Rotate**

　　a　　(b)　　c　　d　　　　　　(a)

4. **Rotate**

　　(a)　　b　　c　　d　　　　　　(a)

Find the figure on the right which is **most like** the three figures on the left.

5.

　(a)　b　(x)　d　e　　　a　　(_)

6.

　a　b　c　(d)　e　　　　　(e)

7.

　a　b　(c)　d　e　　　　　(d)

8.

　a　(b)　c　d　e　　　　　(C)

The third figure is transformed in the same way as the first. Find the figure it **transforms into**.

9.

　a　b　(c)　d　e　　　　　(c)

10.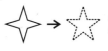

　a　b　(c)　d　e　　　　　(c)

11.

　a　(b)　c　d　e　　　　　(c)

12.

　a　b　c　d　e　　　　　(c)

/12

NHRDE1

11+ Non-Verbal Reasoning — Benchmark Test

There are 36 questions in this test and it should take about 20 minutes. Find the answer to each question and write its letter on the line. If you get stuck on a question, move on to the next one.

Section One

Find the figure in each row that is **most unlike** the other figures.

1.

   a   b   c   d   e   (__)

2.

   a   b   c   d   e   (__)

3.

   a   b   c   d   e   (__)

4.

   a   b   c   d   e   (__)

Find which one of the four squares **completes the sequence** on the left.

5.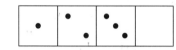

                         a   b   c   d   (__)

6.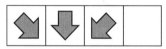

                         a   b   c   d   (__)

7.

                         a   b   c   d   (__)

8.

                         a   b   c   d   (__)

Find the figure on the right which is **most like** the two figures on the left.

9.

                         a   b   c   d   (__)

10.

                         a   b   c   d   (__)

11.

                         a   b   c   d   (__)

12.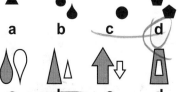

                         a   b   c   d   (__)

/12

NHRDE1

Non-Verbal Reasoning

The 11+ Study Book

and Parents' Guide

Practise • Prepare • Pass

Everything your child needs for 11+ success

9112000034417

CONTENTS

Question Types

Similarities and Differences

Pairs, Series and Grids

Rotation and Reflection

3D Shapes

Published by CGP

Editors:
Gordon Henderson, Anthony Muller, Rebecca Tate and Ben Train.

With thanks to Glenn Rogers and Judy Hornigold for the proofreading.

Please note that CGP is not associated with CEM or The University of Durham in any way.
This book does not include any official questions and it is not endorsed by CEM or The University of Durham.
CEM, Centre for Evaluation and Monitoring, Durham University and
The University of Durham are all trademarks of The University of Durham.

ISBN: 978 1 84762 565 6
Printed by Elanders Ltd, Newcastle upon Tyne.
Clipart from Corel®

Based on the classic CGP style created by Richard Parsons.

What's in the 11+

Make sure you've got your head around the basics of the 11+ before you begin.

The 11+ is an Admissions Test

1) The 11+ is a test used by <u>some schools</u> to help with their <u>selection process</u>.
2) You'll usually take it when you're in <u>Year 6</u>, at some point during the <u>autumn term</u>.
3) Schools <u>use the results</u> to decide who to accept. They might also use <u>other things</u> to help make up their mind, like information about <u>where you live</u>.

If you're unsure, ask your parents to check when you'll be taking your 11+ tests.

You'll be tested on a Mixture of Subjects

1) In your 11+, you'll be tested on <u>these subjects</u>:

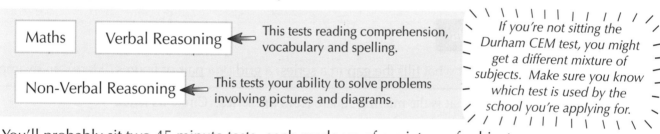

Maths

Verbal Reasoning ← This tests reading comprehension, vocabulary and spelling.

Non-Verbal Reasoning ← This tests your ability to solve problems involving pictures and diagrams.

If you're not sitting the Durham CEM test, you might get a different mixture of subjects. Make sure you know which test is used by the school you're applying for.

2) You'll probably sit <u>two 45 minute tests</u>, each made up of a mixture of subjects.
3) This book will help you with the <u>Non-Verbal Reasoning</u> part of the test.

Get to Know what Kind of Paper you're taking

Your paper will either be <u>multiple choice</u> or <u>standard answer</u>.

Multiple Choice

1) For each question you'll be given some <u>options</u> on a <u>separate answer sheet</u>.
2) You'll need to mark your answer with a <u>clear pencil line</u> in the box next to the <u>option</u> that you think is <u>correct</u>.

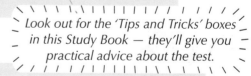

Look out for the 'Tips and Tricks' boxes in this Study Book — they'll give you practical advice about the test.

Standard Answer

1) You'll need to <u>write down</u> or <u>circle</u> the correct letter, or shade in a <u>box</u> under it.
2) You'll still have the same <u>letters</u> to choose from, though.

Check which type of <u>question paper</u> you'll be taking, so you know what it <u>looks</u> like and <u>where</u> your answers go. Try to do some practice tests in the <u>same format</u> as the test you'll be taking, so you know what to <u>expect</u> on the day.

What's in the 11+ Non-Verbal Reasoning Test

Get your brain ready for Non-Verbal Reasoning by reading about the different question types.

Non-Verbal Reasoning involves Solving Problems

1) Non-Verbal Reasoning is about <u>shapes</u> and <u>patterns</u>.
2) Here are a few different <u>question types</u> that could crop up. We've grouped them into <u>categories</u>:

Similarities and Differences

You'll need to spot <u>similarities</u> and <u>differences</u> between <u>different figures</u>. Here's an example:

Q Find the figure that is most like the two figures on the left. Circle its letter.

a   b   c   d

They all have a black shape that's the same as the white shape, and the same way up.

Pairs, Series and Grids

You'll need to work out what <u>fills the gap</u> in a <u>series</u>, a <u>grid</u> or a <u>pair</u> of figures. Here's an example:

Q Find the figure that is the missing square from the series. Circle its letter.

a   b   c   d

There's a grey, six-pointed star moving clockwise round the corners of the square.

Reflection and Rotation

You'll need to work out what shapes look like if they're <u>reflected</u> or <u>rotated</u>. Here's an example:

Q Work out which option would look like the figure on the left if it was rotated. Circle its letter.

a   b   c   d

D is a 90 degree clockwise rotation. A and C are different shapes and the arrow in B is a different colour.

3D Shapes

You'll need to <u>rotate</u> or <u>combine</u> 3D shapes, or <u>imagine</u> them in <u>2D</u>. Here's an example:

Q Work out which option is a top-down 2D view of the 3D figure on the left. Circle its letter.

a   b   c   d

The shape has two blocks at the front of the figure and two blocks at the back with a gap between them.

How to Prepare for the 11+

Give yourself a head start with your Non-Verbal Reasoning preparation — be organised and plan ahead.

Divide your *Preparation* into *Stages*

1) You should find a way to prepare for the 11+ that <u>suits you</u>. This may depend on <u>how much time</u> you have before the test. Here's a good way to <u>plan</u> your Non-Verbal Reasoning practice:

> Do the Benchmark Test at the front of this book. Ask an adult to mark it for you.
>
> Learn strategies for answering different question types using this Study Book.
>
> Do plenty of practice questions, concentrating on the question types you find tricky.
>
> Sit some practice papers to prepare you for the real test.

2) When you <u>first</u> start answering Non-Verbal Reasoning questions, try to solve the questions without <u>making any mistakes</u>, rather than working <u>quickly</u>.

3) Once you feel <u>confident</u> about the questions, then you can build up your <u>speed</u>.

4) You can do this by asking an adult to <u>time</u> you as you answer a <u>set of questions</u>, or by seeing <u>how many</u> questions you can answer in a certain <u>amount of time</u>, e.g. 5 minutes. You can then try to <u>beat</u> your time or score.

5) As you get closer to the test day, work on getting a <u>balance</u> between <u>speed</u> and <u>accuracy</u> — that's what you're <u>aiming for</u> when you sit the real test.

There are *Many Ways* to *Practise* the *Skills* you *Need*

The <u>best way</u> to tackle Non-Verbal Reasoning is to do lots of <u>practice</u>. This isn't the only thing that will help though — there are other ways you can <u>build up the skills</u> you need for the test:

1) Try drawing different <u>shapes</u> on a piece of paper. Use a <u>small mirror</u> to investigate what they look like when they've been <u>reflected</u>.

2) Copy shapes onto <u>tracing paper</u> to look at how different shapes <u>change</u> when you <u>rotate</u> them. This will help you to <u>spot changes quickly</u>.

3) Do activities like <u>jigsaw puzzles</u>, <u>origami</u>, <u>tangrams</u> (see p.15), <u>draughts</u>, <u>sudoku</u> and wooden or metal <u>puzzles</u> to help you to develop your <u>problem-solving skills</u>.

4) Try the <u>warm-up</u> activities on the pages about each question type in this Study Book. They'll introduce you to the kinds of <u>skills</u> you'll use to answer each type of question.

Spotting Patterns

In this section you'll be able to try your hand at all the different parts of Non-Verbal Reasoning. You need to get the hang of everything that can happen in a question if you want to do well.

What you might Have to Do

1) The best way to get good at Non-Verbal Reasoning is to do lots of questions, but first you need to know what you're looking out for. This section will help you get used to spotting the main elements of questions before you get into the details of how each question type works.

2) The real 11+ test will have questions which mix different things together. They won't be split up like they are in this section, but learning about them separately will help you understand how the real questions work.

3) If you get stuck when working through some real 11+ style questions, you can look back at this section to help you understand what's going on.

If you can't solve a question, look at the answer (but not the explanation) and try to work out why it's the right one. If you're still stuck, look at the explanation.

Questions are made up of Different Parts

This section is a good place to start if you're new to Non-Verbal Reasoning or if you want extra practice, because it deals with all the things you'll come across in full 11+ questions.

Even if you're confident about an element, you can use the practice questions for some extra practice.

Learn about and practise Each of the Elements Separately

1) Shapes — the different shapes, the importance of different numbers of sides, and symmetry.

2) Counting — when to count, what to count, and how to use basic maths.

3) Pointing — how arrows can point in directions, as well as at, or away from, an object.

4) Shading and Line Types — the different line types and shadings that a shape can have.

5) Position — where a shape is positioned in a figure.

6) Order — what an order is and how it works if the objects in an order move or change.

7) Rotation — how much an object is turned (its angle) and in what direction.

8) Reflection — when a mirror image of a shape is made by reflecting it across a mirror line.

9) Layering — how and in what ways shapes can overlap.

Some equipment will Help you Understand the Different Elements

1) As you're going through this book, you may find it helpful to have a pen, a pencil and some scrap paper. Doing a rough drawing of how you think a figure should look in questions that you're struggling with might help you work out the answer.

2) A protractor might help you see the angle and direction a figure is turned. If you have an analogue clock or watch, this might also help with clockwise and anticlockwise directions.

3) A mirror will help you understand reflection and symmetry.

4) Once you've got to grips with the basics in this book, you should put everything away apart from a pen, pencil and rough paper, as you won't be able to use the other things in the real test.

Shapes

Shapes are everywhere in Non-Verbal Reasoning. To do well, you'll need to get really good at spotting the similarities and differences between them.

Warm-Up Activity

Cut a square, a triangle and a circle out of a piece of scrap paper. See how many <u>different ways</u> you can <u>fold</u> each one in <u>half</u> so both sides are exactly the <u>same</u>.

Shapes have different *Numbers* of *Sides*

You can tell what <u>type of shape</u> something is by how <u>many sides</u> it has, so you should always count the <u>number</u> of sides of different <u>shapes</u> in a question.

Shapes of the *Same Type* can *Look Different*

1) Even though the shapes below have the same number of sides, they look <u>different</u>. That's because their <u>sides</u> are different <u>lengths</u> or their <u>angles</u> are different.

These shapes are all triangles...

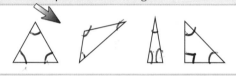

... and these are all rectangles.

2) Some shapes will look really <u>different</u>, but they might still have the <u>same</u> number of sides.

These are all quadrilaterals — they have four sides.

These are all hexagons — they have six sides.

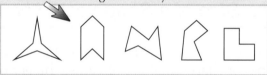

You'll need to *Count* the *Sides* of different shapes

Some questions use <u>sequences</u> based on the <u>number of sides</u> that shapes have.

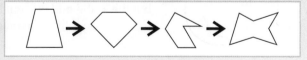

In this example, the number of sides goes up by one each time — four, five, six and seven.

Some shapes have *Curved Sides*

Don't forget to count <u>curved sides</u> as well.

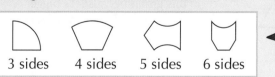

3 sides   4 sides   5 sides   6 sides

Look out for questions where you only need to look at the number of curved sides. In this example, the five-sided shape is different to the others because it's the only one with two curved sides.

Spotting Patterns

The **Sides** of a **Shape** could be **Important**

For some questions you will have to spot which shapes are <u>similar</u> and which are <u>different</u>.

Shapes might be different because they have **Different Numbers** of **Sides**

Sometimes you'll need to spot a shape that has a different <u>number of sides</u> from the rest. This can be <u>tricky</u> if all the shapes look very <u>different</u>.

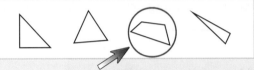

The third shape is the odd one out because it has four sides, not three.

Shapes might be different because they have **Different Lengths** of **Sides**

You might have to spot <u>one different</u> shape in a group that all have the <u>same</u> <u>number</u> of sides. Look for shapes with different <u>angles</u> or sides of different <u>lengths</u>.

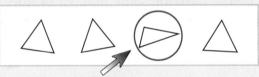

These shapes are all triangles, but the third one is different. Its sides are different lengths — the other triangles all have three sides of equal length.

The **Size** of a **Shape** could be **Important**

You can compare the <u>size</u> of <u>any shapes</u>, even if they're <u>completely different</u>. Look for shapes that are <u>obviously bigger</u> or <u>smaller</u> than the rest.

1) A <u>shape</u> might be a <u>different size</u> to other shapes, even though it has the same number of sides. This can be quite easy to spot if the other <u>shapes</u> are all the <u>same</u>.

These shapes all have five sides, but this is the odd one out because it's bigger than the others.

2) <u>Different shapes</u> might be the <u>same size</u>, even if they have <u>different numbers</u> <u>of sides</u>. When the numbers of sides are all different, they <u>won't help you</u> spot the odd one out — you'll need to look for <u>another difference</u>.

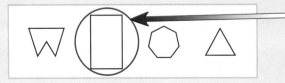

The rectangle is the odd one out in this group because it's bigger than the other shapes, which are all about the same size.

Some shapes are **Symmetrical**

A shape is <u>symmetrical</u> if you can <u>draw</u> a <u>line</u> through it that <u>divides</u> the shape into <u>halves</u> which are <u>mirror images</u> of each other.

1) Imagine that the shape is <u>folded in half</u> along a line that goes through the middle of the shape. If the two sides fit together <u>exactly</u>, the shape is symmetrical.

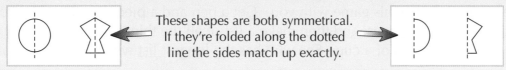

These shapes are both symmetrical. If they're folded along the dotted line the sides match up exactly.

2) If the two halves aren't <u>exactly</u> the same, the shape <u>isn't symmetrical</u>.

No matter where you fold this shape, the two halves don't match up.

You'll often have to think about **More Than One** shape

1) Sometimes the <u>type of shape</u> won't be important — you'll need to look at other things like <u>shading</u>, or whether its <u>outline</u> is solid, dotted or dashed (see p.12-14).

2) For a lot of questions, you'll have to think about <u>other things</u>, such as — Do the shapes have <u>different rotations</u>? What is their <u>total number</u> of <u>sides</u>? How are they <u>positioned</u> in <u>relation</u> to <u>other objects</u>?

Practice Questions

1) Which shape is the odd one out? Circle the right letter.

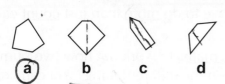
    a   b   c   d

If any of these questions don't make sense, check out the different question types on p.30, p.33 and p.40.

2) Which shape is the most like the first two shapes? Circle the right letter.

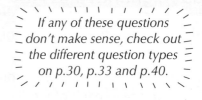
            a   b   c   d

3) Which shape comes next in the series? Circle the right letter.

      a   b   c   d

Counting

If in doubt, count everything — shapes, sides, dots and lines. The solution to a tricky-looking question could be as simple as how many of something there are.

Warm-Up Activity

Find another person to play this game with you. Get a pen and a piece of paper for each of you. Set a timer for two minutes, and then make a list of all the things you can see that are circles, e.g. a coin or the top of a cup. See who has the longest list when the time is up.

You'll **Often** need to **Count Things**

In easier questions it might be as simple as counting to four.

1) For some figures it will be obvious what you should count.

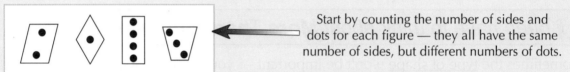

Start by counting the number of sides and dots for each figure — they all have the same number of sides, but different numbers of dots.

2) For others it will be less obvious what you should count.

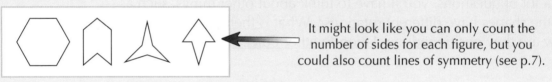

It might look like you can only count the number of sides for each figure, but you could also count lines of symmetry (see p.7).

You might have to **Add** or **Subtract**

If there is more than one type of object, you sometimes have to do more than just count each one.

1) For harder questions you'll need to do some basic maths to work out how two numbers relate to each other. Look for relationships between the different things you can count.

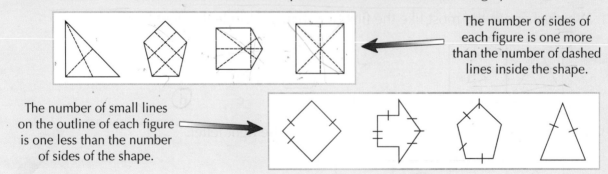

The number of sides of each figure is one more than the number of dashed lines inside the shape.

The number of small lines on the outline of each figure is one less than the number of sides of the shape.

2) Keep track of all the numbers of different elements in each figure. You'll find the answer to some questions by noticing that there is a pattern in the difference between two of these numbers, or in their total when added together.

Spotting Patterns

Equal Numbers of Different Objects could be Important

<u>Add different elements</u> together to see if their <u>total</u> is <u>equal</u> to the number of <u>another element</u>.

If you're looking for <u>connections</u> between figures, try <u>every counting combination</u>.

For these figures, you could count circles, squares, sides and lines (among other things).

In all these figures the <u>number of lines added</u> to the <u>number of small shapes</u> is the <u>same</u> as the <u>number of sides</u> of the <u>large shape</u>.

You might also have to notice when different figures all have an odd or even number of objects.

[handwritten]
Shap 4   2   2   2
sides 6   4   5   3
line 2   2   2   1

Counting is Important in Series Questions

You will often have to <u>add</u> or <u>subtract</u> for series questions.

<u>Counting</u> will tell you how <u>many</u> of each thing are added or subtracted, so you can work out what should come <u>next</u>.

See p.40 for more on Series Questions.

The star is losing a point in each figure, but gaining a dot. The next figure will have three points and five dots.

7 points, 1 dot   6 points, 2 dots   5 points, 3 dots   4 points, 4 dots

Practice Questions

1) Which figure is the odd one out? Circle the right letter.

[handwritten]
No of sides   4   6   5   3   2
dotes   3   3   1   2   4
lines   3   2   1   2   4

    a   b   c   d   e

2) Which figure is the most like the first two figures? Circle the right letter.

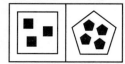

                a   b   c   d

3) Which figure comes next in the series? Circle the right letter.

                                  a   b   c   d

Pointing

Don't just look at what arrows are pointing at — it might also be important
what an arrow is pointing away from, or what direction it's pointing in.

Warm-Up Activity

Cut a circle and an arrow out of card. Using a pen, divide the circle
into six equal sections, and number them from one to six. Make a hole
in the middle of the circle and the arrow, then use a split pin to attach
them together. Try using your spinner instead of a dice in a board game.

Arrows Point in a Direction

Arrows can point up, down, left and right, as well as diagonally,
so you need to look at the exact direction an arrow is pointing.

1) It helps to know the different directions that an arrow can point.

2) You need to notice when arrows point in the same direction or a different direction.

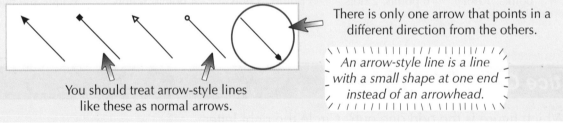

You should treat arrow-style lines like these as normal arrows.

There is only one arrow that points in a different direction from the others.

An arrow-style line is a line with a small shape at one end instead of an arrowhead.

Arrows can Point At Objects

As well as direction, you should also check if an arrow is pointing towards or away from something.

1) You need to look at what an arrow is pointing at.

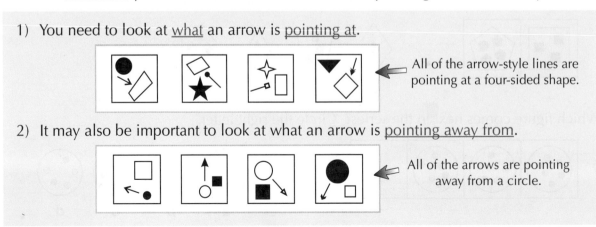

All of the arrow-style lines are pointing at a four-sided shape.

2) It may also be important to look at what an arrow is pointing away from.

All of the arrows are pointing away from a circle.

Arrows *can point* **Clockwise** *or* **Anticlockwise**

Not all arrows just <u>point</u> in a <u>straight line</u> — some arrows also <u>go</u> in a <u>circular direction</u>.

1) <u>Clockwise</u> means the <u>direction</u> in which the <u>hands</u> on a <u>clock move</u>. <u>Anticlockwise</u> means the <u>opposite direction</u>.

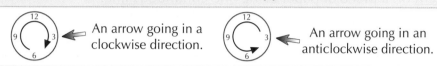

An arrow going in a clockwise direction.

An arrow going in an anticlockwise direction.

2) All these arrows point in a <u>clockwise direction</u>.

Both straight arrows with corners and curved arrows can point in a clockwise or anticlockwise direction.

3) All these arrows point in an <u>anticlockwise direction</u>.

It might help you work out if an arrow is going clockwise or anticlockwise if you imagine it going round an invisible clock face.

4) Arrows <u>next to shapes</u> can also suggest a <u>clockwise</u> or <u>anticlockwise direction</u>.

The figures with anticlockwise arrows are circled in red.

Practice Questions

1) Which figure is the odd one out? Circle the right letter.

   a   **b**   **c**   **d**   **e**

2) Which arrow comes next in the series? Circle the right letter.

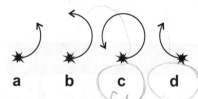

   a   **b**   **c**   **d**

3) Which arrow is the most like the first two arrows? Circle the right letter.

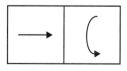

   a   **b**   **c**   **d**

Shading and Line Types

Every shape that you come across will be drawn with a particular type of line, and shaded in a particular way. Recognising different line types and shadings will be an important skill for the test.

Warm-Up Activity

Draw a <u>scribble pattern</u> on a piece of paper using <u>one continuous line</u>. Using as <u>few</u> coloured pencils as possible, colour each shape in your scribble pattern so that <u>no two shapes</u> with <u>touching sides</u> (corners are okay) share the <u>same shading</u>.

It's possible to colour in all scribble patterns like this using only four colours.

Shapes can be Shaded in Different Ways

There are a few <u>main ways</u> that shapes are shaded.

There are other weird shadings that sometimes appear. If you come across any, don't be put off — treat them like any other type of shading.

Look out for the <u>most common types</u>:

|  White | Black | Grey |  Hatched | Spotted |

There are Different Types of Hatching

Hatching is when shapes are shaded with lines.

It's not always enough to <u>notice</u> that a shape is <u>hatched</u> — you also need to look at <u>how</u> it is hatched.

Check the Direction of the Hatching

It's easy to miss <u>different types</u> of hatching unless you <u>check</u> each hatched shape <u>carefully</u>.

These shapes are all hatched in different directions.

 Vertical hatching   Horizontal hatching   Hatching going diagonally down to the left.   Hatching going diagonally down to the right.

Look out for Unusual Hatching

You could even get a question where the number of hatched lines is important.

You might get a shape that is <u>hatched</u> in an <u>unusual way</u> — just treat it like <u>any other</u> hatched shape.

These shapes are also hatched, but with different types of hatching.  Cross-hatched   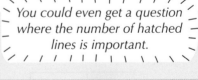 Thick hatching    White hatching on a black shape

Different Shapes might share the *Same Shading*

When there are lots of shaded shapes, you could look for shapes that are shaded the same.

1) If the answer to a question is about the shading of large shapes it might be obvious.

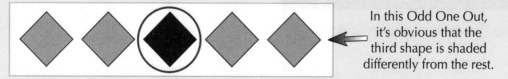

In this Odd One Out, it's obvious that the third shape is shaded differently from the rest.

2) If the answer to a question focuses on the shading of more than one shape, or a smaller part of a figure, it might be trickier to spot.

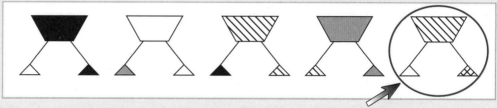

This Odd One Out is quite tricky, but by checking all the shapes and comparing them, you can work out the answer. The fifth figure is the only one with a small right-hand shape shaded differently from the large shape.

The *Amount* a *Shape* is *Shaded* could be *Important*

Different parts of shapes can be shaded, but the total amount of shading might be the same. You might need to work out what fraction of a shape is shaded.

1) Sometimes you will need to use basic maths to work out how much is shaded.

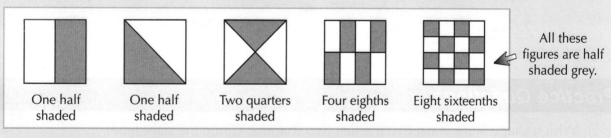

One half shaded · One half shaded · Two quarters shaded · Four eighths shaded · Eight sixteenths shaded

All these figures are half shaded grey.

2) You might have to add two different amounts of shading together.

The shading of these two figures added together equals one whole shape.

The shading of these two figures added together equals three quarters of a whole shape.

3) You might have to work out how much shading needs to be added or taken away from a figure.

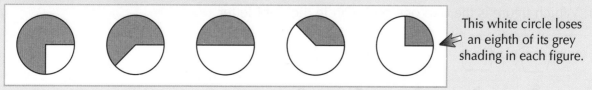

This white circle loses an eighth of its grey shading in each figure.

Spotting Patterns

Lines *can be* **Drawn Differently**

The lines of <u>figures</u>, <u>arrows</u> and the <u>outlines</u> on shapes can be <u>different line types</u> and <u>styles</u>. You don't need to <u>remember</u> them, but you need to be able to <u>spot</u> which lines are <u>different</u> in a question.

Check for **Different Line Types** *and* **Styles**

1) These are the most common <u>line types</u>.

| Solid line | Dashed line | Dotted line | Thin solid line | Thick solid line | Long-dashed line | Short-dashed line |

2) Lines also come in <u>different styles</u>.

| Straight line | Curved line | Wavy line | Jagged line |

Other line thicknesses and lengths of line dashes might come up, but you only need to be able to spot the differences between different lines.

3) You'll see <u>all sorts</u> of combinations of <u>line types</u> and <u>styles</u>.

| Thin solid straight line | Thick solid curved line | Short-dashed wavy line | Dotted jagged line | Thick long-dashed curved line |

Watch out for shapes with **Different Lengths** *of* **Dashes** *in their* **Outline**

The <u>number of lines</u> used to <u>draw</u> a shape isn't always the <u>same</u> as its <u>number of sides</u>.

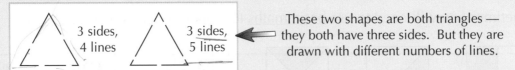

3 sides, 4 lines   3 sides, 5 lines

These two shapes are both triangles — they both have three sides. But they are drawn with different numbers of lines.

Practice Questions

1) Which shape is the most like the first two shapes? Circle the right letter.

                             a   **b**   **c**   **d**

2) Which figure comes next in the series? Circle the right letter.

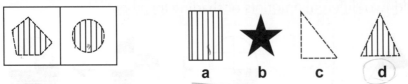

                  a   **b**   **c**   **d**

3) Which figure is the odd one out? Circle the right letter.

   a   **b**   **c**   **d**   **e**

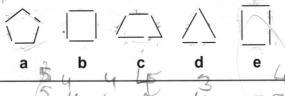

Spotting Patterns

Position

Position is all about where something is — whether an object is at the top, the bottom, the left or the right of a figure — and it could be important in working out the answer to a question.

Warm-Up Activity

Trace over the shapes on the right and draw them on a new piece of paper. Position the shapes together to make different shapes. Can you use all of the shapes and make them into one complete square?

This is called a tangram.

Every Object has a Position

Noticing <u>where</u> something is sounds <u>simple</u>, but it's easy to <u>miss something obvious</u>.

Objects can have <u>similar</u> or <u>different positions</u>. <u>Keeping track</u> of <u>each shape's position</u> helps you <u>spot similarities</u> and <u>differences</u>.

Taken together, the position of both the rectangle and the star is not the same in any of these figures, but in all of the figures the rectangle is always at the top, and the star is always on the left.

Objects also have a Position in Relation to Other Objects

When there's <u>more</u> than <u>one shape</u>, each object has a <u>position</u> other than just its <u>own</u>.

1) Two <u>objects</u> may be in <u>different positions</u> in different figures, but in the same position in <u>relation</u> to <u>each other</u>.

The trapezium and the spot are in different positions in each figure, but the spot is directly above the trapezium in all the figures.

2) In harder questions where there are <u>more than two</u> objects, you will need to look at the position of <u>each object</u> in relation to <u>all</u> the <u>other objects</u>.

In this Odd One Out, the circle is to the left of the cross in every figure except for the fifth one. The square's position doesn't matter.

Objects can **Move Position** in a **Sequence**

You might have to work out <u>how</u> an object is moving so you can decide <u>where</u> it should be <u>next</u>. Some object movements are <u>more common</u> than others.

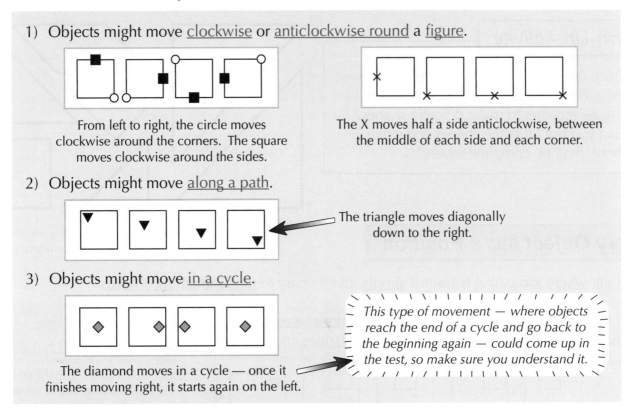

1) Objects might move <u>clockwise</u> or <u>anticlockwise round</u> a <u>figure</u>.

From left to right, the circle moves clockwise around the corners. The square moves clockwise around the sides.

The X moves half a side anticlockwise, between the middle of each side and each corner.

2) Objects might move <u>along a path</u>.

The triangle moves diagonally down to the right.

3) Objects might move <u>in a cycle</u>.

The diamond moves in a cycle — once it finishes moving right, it starts again on the left.

This type of movement — where objects reach the end of a cycle and go back to the beginning again — could come up in the test, so make sure you understand it.

The **Position** of **New Objects** is **Important**

When an object is <u>added</u> to a figure you need to look at <u>where</u> the <u>new object</u> is <u>positioned</u>.

1) Once you've worked out <u>what</u> is being <u>added</u>, you need to work out <u>where</u> it is added.

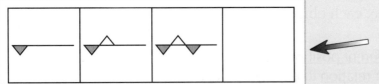

In this Series question, grey triangles and white triangles are added in turn. The missing square must have an extra white triangle, and it must be above the line on the right-hand side of the figure.

All of these figures have the right number of triangles in the right colours, but only the third figure has the extra white triangle in the correct position.

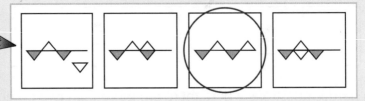

2) In some questions, <u>two or more</u> figures are <u>added together</u> to make a <u>third figure</u>.

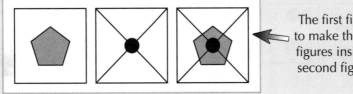

The first figure is added to the second figure to make the third figure. The position of both figures inside the square stays the same. The second figure goes in front of the first figure.

The **Position** of objects that are **Removed** can be **Important**

It's not enough to notice when something is <u>removed</u> — you need to notice <u>where</u> it's <u>removed from</u>.

1) Objects or parts of an object can be <u>removed</u> in <u>different ways</u> and <u>from different positions</u>.

In this Series question the circle loses a sixth each time, so the next square must have a circle fraction of two sixths. The circle always loses the sixth going in a clockwise direction, so the next sixth must be removed from the left-hand side of the semicircle.

All these figures have the correct circle fraction, but only the fourth figure has it in the correct position.

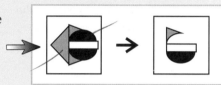

2) Even if <u>two figures</u> are <u>not the same</u>, you can see what objects should be <u>removed</u> by looking at their <u>positions</u>.

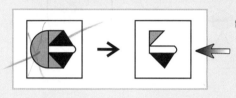

For both of these pairs, to get from the first figure to the second remove the top black shape, the bottom grey shape and the left-hand shape.

Practice Questions

1) Which figure comes next in the series? Circle the right letter.

        a   b   c   d

2) Which figure is the odd one out? Circle the right letter.

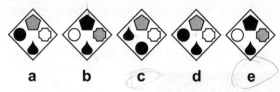

     a   b   c   d   e

3) Which figure comes next in the series? Circle the right letter.

       a   b   c   d

Order

When you arrange two or more objects into a group or line, you've put them in an order.

Warm-Up Activity

Find three different coins and see how many different orders you can line them up in.

Objects can be **Arranged** in a **Particular Order**

Any group of shapes in a line can be seen as having an order.

You might have to spot whether orders of shapes are the same or different.

All these figures are in the same order except for the circled figure, where the circle and the hexagon have swapped places.

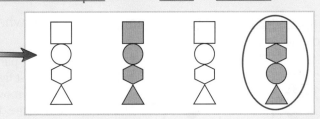

Some orders are the **Same** but **Look Different**

Shapes don't have to be in the same positions to be in the same order.

Choose a **Starting Point** to **Check** an order

1) You can check if an order is the same by starting with the same object and then counting the rest of the objects in turn.

All these figures go from left to right in the order: triangle, diamond, pentagon, except for the circled figure.

2) When you reach the end of a line of shapes (in this case the right) you should continue from the other end (in this case the left), until you have gone through every shape.

Objects can move but keep the same order. You might have to work out how each object is moving.

If an **Order Moves** check **What Happens** to the **End Object**

If all the objects in a line of shapes move positions in the same way, the end object moves to the beginning of the order.

All of these shapes have moved one place to the right. When a shape cannot move any further right, it appears again on the left.

The movement just means the order starts with a different shape. If the objects moved another place to the right they'd be arranged: X shape, heart, circle, triangle (from left to right).

Objects can be **Ordered Around** a **Shape**

Objects round a shape might have a <u>clockwise</u> or an <u>anticlockwise arrangement</u>.

1) Pick a <u>starting point</u> and <u>work round</u> the shape in the <u>same direction</u> to <u>check the order</u>.

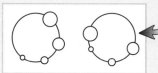

In this Odd One Out the shapes in the second figure are arranged in a different order from the rest. It goes circle, star, square, triangle in a clockwise direction. (The rest go circle, star, triangle, square.)

2) Different figures can have the <u>same circular order</u> but they might <u>look different</u>.

These two figures have the same order. The circles are in size order, from biggest to smallest, going in a clockwise direction.

This figure looks similar, but it's arranged in size order, from biggest to smallest, going in an anticlockwise direction.

There might be **More Than One Order** in a question

If there is <u>more than one order</u>, and each order <u>moves about</u>, it can be <u>hard to spot</u> what's going on.

1) <u>Shading</u> is often used as a <u>separate order</u>, for example:

The order stays the same for both shading and shapes, but the orders have moved.

2) To work out how the <u>two orders move</u> you can <u>separate them</u>.

All the shapes move one place to the left. It goes from triangle, square, circle to square, circle, triangle.

All the shadings move one place to the right. It goes from black, cross-hatched, hatched to hatched, black, cross-hatched.

Practice Questions

1) Which figure is the odd one out? Circle the right letter.

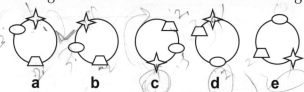

a   b   c   d   e

2) Which figure comes next in the series? Circle the right letter.

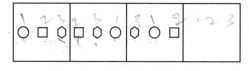

a   b   c   d

Rotation

Rotation is when an object is turned, either around its own centre, or around another point.

Warm-Up Activity

Draw a <u>picture</u> on a piece of paper. <u>Without turning</u> the page, try drawing how you think the picture would look <u>upside down</u> on a separate piece of paper. <u>Turn</u> the original piece of paper round to see how <u>close</u> you got.

Rotation is when a Shape is Turned

An object can be <u>turned</u> in <u>different ways</u>, and it will <u>often look different</u> after it has been <u>rotated</u>.

<u>Different rotations</u> of a shape look <u>different</u> from <u>each other</u>.

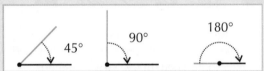

This is the same shape rotated six times. Each figure looks different because it's rotated a different amount (or angle).

Shapes can rotate Different Amounts and in Different Directions

Objects can rotate in a <u>clockwise</u> or <u>anticlockwise direction</u>.

See p.11 for more on clockwise and anticlockwise directions.

There are lots of **Different Angles**

1) You'll need to recognise these <u>angles of rotation</u>, and work out the <u>correct direction</u>.

 45° 90° 180°

 Clockwise Anticlockwise

2) Knowing about <u>angles</u> will help you work out <u>how much</u> a shape is rotated.

 45°    90°   180°

The shape is rotated clockwise in each example.

Series Questions *often use* **Rotation**

Some shapes look the same when they are rotated 180 degrees — for example the first and fifth figures.

This shows how shapes might <u>rotate</u> in a <u>series question</u>.

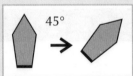   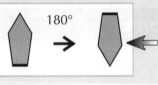

This figure is rotated 90 degrees clockwise each time.

This figure is rotated 45 degrees anticlockwise each time.

Spotting Patterns

Rotation **Disguises** whether shapes are the **Same** or **Different**

Rotation can make shapes <u>look different</u>, even when they are the <u>same</u>.

It can be <u>even harder</u> to see whether a <u>complicated shape</u> has been rotated.

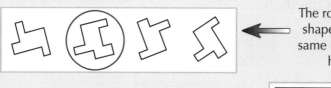

The rotation makes it hard to spot that the second shape is different. Picking a point that looks the same in each shape and following the edge might help you see if each shape is the same.

Only the fifth figure is the same as the first two — but the rotation makes all the figures look similar.

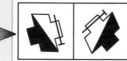 

Turning the page so that a particular part of a figure is at the top might help you recognise similar shapes.

Parts of a figure might **Rotate** on their **Own**

The <u>different parts</u> of a figure don't have to <u>rotate together</u> — a <u>part</u> might rotate <u>on its own</u>, or in a <u>different way</u> to the <u>rest of the figure</u>.

1) In a <u>complicated figure</u>, only a <u>small part</u> might <u>rotate</u> (often other things will be happening).

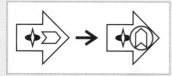   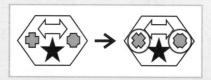

Only the small white arrowhead is rotated — the rest of the figure stays the same.

Only the small grey shapes are rotated — the rest of the figure stays the same.

2) Sometimes <u>part</u> of a figure will <u>rotate round another part</u> of the figure.

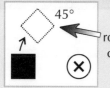

This square rotates 45 degrees clockwise round the circle.

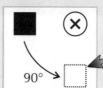

This square rotates 90 degrees anticlockwise round the circle.

This square rotates 180 degrees round the circle — it could be in either direction.

Different Objects might **Rotate Differently**

In harder questions, you need to check the rotation of <u>each object separately</u>.

If you <u>assume</u> that everything is <u>rotating</u> in the <u>same way</u> you could make a <u>mistake</u>.

The black shape rotates 45 degrees anticlockwise each time.

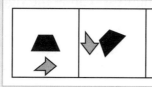 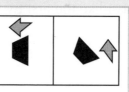

The grey shape rotates 90 degrees clockwise around the black shape.

Hatched Shapes *have* Complicated *rotations*

Because <u>hatching</u> is made up of <u>angled lines</u> it can also be <u>rotated</u>.

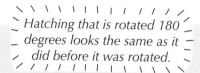

Hatching that is rotated 180 degrees looks the same as it did before it was rotated.

1) You should check <u>hatched shading carefully</u>, because it might not <u>rotate</u> in the <u>same way</u> as the shape.

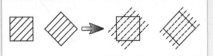 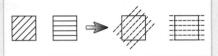

The square rotates, but the hatching stays the same.

The hatching rotates, but the square stays the same.

2) If you think the <u>shape</u> and the <u>hatching</u> are rotating <u>differently</u>, you should <u>always</u> <u>double-check</u>. Work out the <u>shape's rotation first</u>, then look at the <u>hatching</u>.

There are two rotations here.

The shape rotates 90 degrees anticlockwise.

The hatching rotates 45 degrees clockwise.

3) <u>Hatching</u> looks the <u>same</u> rotated <u>90 degrees clockwise</u> or <u>90 degrees anticlockwise</u>.

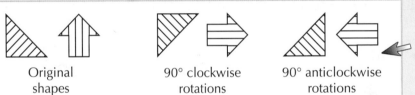

Original shapes

90° clockwise rotations

90° anticlockwise rotations

The hatching rotates with the shape 90 degrees clockwise and 90 degrees anticlockwise, but it looks the same both ways.

Practice Questions

1) Which figure is a rotation of the figure on the left? Circle the right letter.

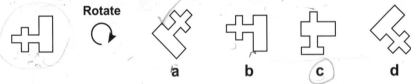

Rotate

a   b   c   d

2) Which figure comes next in the series? Circle the right letter.

a   b   c   d

3) Which figure is the most like the first two figures? Circle the right letter.

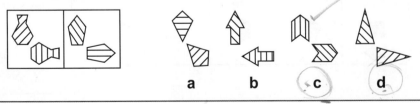

a   b   c   d

Spotting Patterns

Reflection

If you look in a mirror you will see your reflection. Reflecting a shape or an object is the same idea, except that you're doing it on a piece of paper instead of in a mirror.

Warm-Up Activity

Draw a picture on a piece of paper. Then, try to draw how the picture would look if you held it up to a mirror. Use a real mirror to check how close your drawing was to the reflection.

Reflection is when a shape gets Flipped across a Mirror Line

A reflected shape should look like the original shape as if it was seen in a mirror.

Reflections use a *Mirror Line*

1) If you were to put a real mirror along a mirror line you would see in the mirror how the original shape should be reflected.

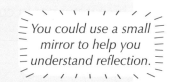
You could use a small mirror to help you understand reflection.

2) The shapes on either side of the mirror line should be identical to each other, except that one has been flipped over.

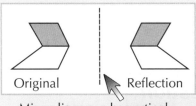

Mirror lines can be vertical...
(Shape is reflected across)

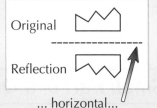

... horizontal...
(Shape is reflected downwards)

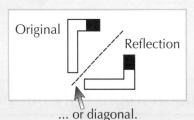

... or diagonal.
(Shape is reflected diagonally)

Most Reflection Questions Won't show you a Mirror Line

Spotting that a shape is reflected is half the battle, so it helps to get used to recognising reflections. Think about how shapes would look if they were reflected.

If you work out where the mirror line should go, it will help you see whether one shape is a reflection of another.

It's obvious that the right-hand figure is a reflection of the left-hand shape.

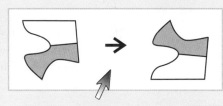

Even though these figures are next to each other, the right-hand shape is a downwards reflection of the left-hand shape.

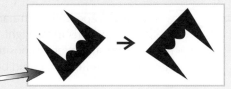

Even though these figures are next to each other, the right-hand shape is a diagonal reflection of the left-hand shape.

A reflection won't always tell you where the shape should be, only what it should look like.

With **Some Shapes** it's **Hard** to **Spot** a **Reflection**

Even simple reflections can be a bit <u>tricky</u> — especially if a <u>hatched shape</u> is involved.

1) Some reflected shapes look the same as the <u>original shape</u>.

This figure has been reflected across the mirror line, but it looks the same on both sides of the dashed line.

This figure has also been reflected, but it also looks the same.

2) <u>Hatched shapes</u> might give you a <u>clue</u> as to whether a <u>shape</u> has been reflected, because <u>hatching</u> can also be <u>reflected</u>.

Shapes that look the same after a reflection must always have at least one line of symmetry.

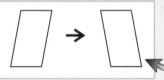

Diagonal hatching looks like it's been rotated 90 degrees if it's reflected across or downwards. If it's reflected diagonally, it will look the same as it does on the original shape.

3) <u>Parallelograms</u> only look <u>slightly different</u> if they are reflected — you should be careful not to confuse a <u>reflected</u> parallelogram with a <u>rotated one</u>.

This figure shows how a parallelogram is reflected — it would look the same if it was reflected downwards or across.

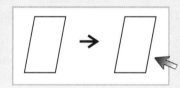

A 180 degree rotation of a parallelogram looks the same as it does before it's rotated.

Reflection might only be a **Small Part** of a **Question**

In <u>complicated questions</u> reflection might only be <u>part</u> of everything that's going on, so you need to <u>check carefully</u> for reflected shapes.

1) In questions where there is a <u>lot happening</u>, it could be <u>easy</u> to <u>miss</u> a <u>reflection</u>.

The bottom shape reflects across in each series square.

2) In some questions you might have to <u>work out</u> how <u>one figure turns into another</u>.

The black shape in the left-hand figure is reflected downwards in the right-hand figure.

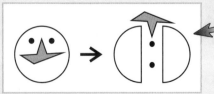

The grey shape in the left-hand figure is reflected upwards in the right-hand figure. Because the shape moves position as well as reflecting, the reflection could be hard to spot.

See p.7 for more on symmetry.

*Be **Careful** not to **Confuse Reflection** with **Rotation***

Rotation and reflection often appear together, so you need to be able to tell the two apart.

*Check that a **Rotation** isn't **Hiding** a **Reflection***

Unsymmetrical figures which are reflected cannot be rotated to match the original figure.

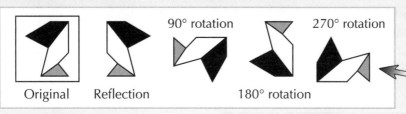

90° rotation   270° rotation

Original   Reflection   180° rotation

No matter how the reflected shape is rotated, it won't look the same as the original.

The circled figure is a reflection of all the other shapes, but this is hidden by its rotation.

*Questions with **Reflected** shapes that **Also Rotate** can be **Tricky***

If a figure rotates and reflects at the same time, it's hard to work out what's happening.

In this sequence the shape rotates 90 degrees anticlockwise each time, then reflects across its longest side. You can tell that it must reflect because no matter how you rotate each shape it won't match the next shape in the sequence.

Practice Questions

1) Which figure is the odd one out? Circle the right letter.

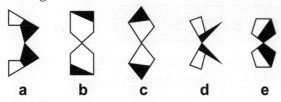

    a   **b**   **c**   **d**   **e**

2) Which figure is a reflection of the figure on the left? Circle the right letter.

Reflect

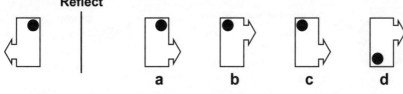

          a   **b**   **c**   **d**

3) Which figure comes next in the series? Circle the right letter.

          a   **b**   **c**   **d**

Layering

Layering is when a shape is in front of or behind another shape. Imagine putting a book on top of another book. If you looked at the pile of books from the side you would see that it has two layers.

Warm-Up Activity

Find <u>five different objects</u> (e.g. a mug, a ruler), as well as a pencil and a piece of paper. <u>Draw around</u> each of the objects so that their <u>outlines overlap</u>. <u>Colour</u> in the parts of your picture where the <u>shapes overlap</u>.

Shapes can **Overlap** in **Different Ways**

You might see <u>all</u> the <u>outlines</u> of <u>overlapping shapes</u>, or one shape might be <u>in front of</u> the other.

1) Even without changing <u>position</u>, <u>two shapes</u> can overlap <u>differently</u>.

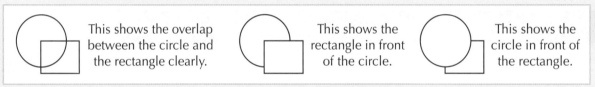

This shows the overlap between the circle and the rectangle clearly.

This shows the rectangle in front of the circle.

This shows the circle in front of the rectangle.

2) The <u>type</u> of <u>overlap</u> shown could be <u>important</u> in a question.

The triangle which is at the front changes — from the bottom triangle, to the middle, to the top.

A shape might move in front of another.   Shapes could be layered differently in a sequence.

The **Shapes Created** by an **Overlap** are **Important**

Try treating the overlap between the two shapes as a <u>separate shape</u>. The shape created by an <u>overlap</u> can look a bit strange, which might help you spot a <u>cut-out shape</u>.

1) When <u>two or more</u> shapes <u>overlap</u>, <u>extra shapes</u> are <u>made</u>.

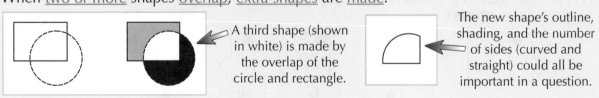

A third shape (shown in white) is made by the overlap of the circle and rectangle.

The new shape's outline, shading, and the number of sides (curved and straight) could all be important in a question.

2) In some questions the overlap will be <u>cut out</u> and <u>changed</u>.

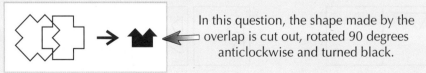

In this question, the shape made by the overlap is cut out, rotated 90 degrees anticlockwise and turned black.

Shapes can be **Ordered** by **Layer**

In questions where shapes <u>overlap</u> it might be important how they are <u>arranged</u> — you should check which shape is at the <u>front</u> and which is at the <u>back</u>.

1) If there are <u>lots</u> of figures that are <u>layered</u>, you could look at what <u>all</u> the shapes at the <u>front</u> or <u>back</u> have in <u>common</u>.

The black shape is at the front of each figure, and the white shape is always at the back.

2) Where <u>two shapes overlap</u> in each figure, the shapes at the <u>front</u> might all be different, but be <u>related</u> to the shapes <u>behind</u> them in the <u>same way</u>.

The shape with the most sides is always at the back — the shape with the fewest sides is always at the front.

Some questions will have **More Than One Overlap**

In questions with <u>lots of overlapping</u> shapes you need to look at <u>more</u> than just the <u>front</u> and <u>back shapes</u> — you also need to look at <u>all</u> the shapes <u>in between</u>.

*Look at how **Shapes** are **Layered** on top of **Each Other***

Overlapping shapes can be <u>positioned</u> in <u>different ways</u>.

These three shapes can be layered in the same order but in different positions.

Going diagonally up to the left. From front to back — black, grey, white.

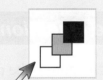

Going diagonally down to the left. From front to back — black, grey, white.

*Look at how **Every Shape** is **Layered** in a figure*

1) Figures can also be layered so that <u>every shape</u> overlaps <u>each other</u>.

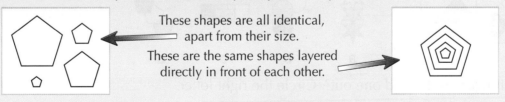

These shapes are all identical, apart from their size.
These are the same shapes layered directly in front of each other.

2) Watch out for figures where <u>every shape</u> is <u>layered</u>, but not every shape <u>overlaps</u>.

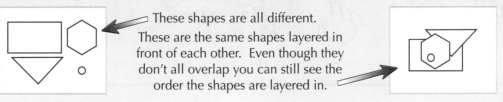

These shapes are all different.
These are the same shapes layered in front of each other. Even though they don't all overlap you can still see the order the shapes are layered in.

Spotting Patterns

Layered *shapes might* Change Position, Layer *or* Colour

If layered shapes <u>change colour</u> or <u>position</u>, you should <u>double check</u> whether the <u>order</u> of the shapes <u>stays the same</u> or not.

1) Sometimes <u>layered shapes</u> will <u>change</u> without moving.

These shapes stay in the same position, but the shading moves back (or out) one shape each time.

2) Sometimes layered shapes will <u>move positions</u> or <u>layers</u>.

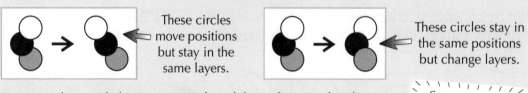

These circles move positions but stay in the same layers.

These circles stay in the same positions but change layers.

3) Because layered shapes are <u>ordered</u> from <u>front to back</u> they can also <u>move layers</u> and still be in the <u>same order</u>.

See p.18-19 for more about order.

Although all of these figures move positions and layers, they still have the same order — C shape, rectangle, arrow-style line, triangle — they just have different shapes at the front.

Practice Questions

1) Which figure is the odd one out? Circle the right letter.

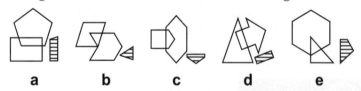

    a   **b**   **c**   **d**   **e**

2) Which figure is the most like the first two figures? Circle the right letter.

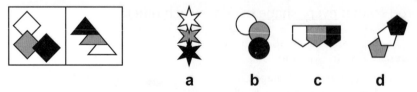

         a   **b**   **c**   **d**

3) Which figure is the odd one out? Circle the right letter.

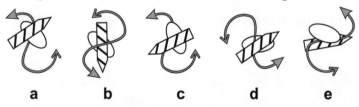

    a   **b**   **c**   **d**   **e**

Similarities and Differences

The questions on this page are all about finding a figure that's the same as or different from another group of figures. They're a bit like spot the difference puzzles... only different.

You'll need to **Compare** different figures

1) These questions are all about spotting <u>similarities</u> and <u>differences</u> between figures.

2) To find the right answer, you'll have to <u>compare</u> the different <u>elements</u> of the figures, like shading or shape. Look back at pages 4-28 to <u>remind</u> yourself what to look for.

3) There are <u>two</u> types of question in this section:

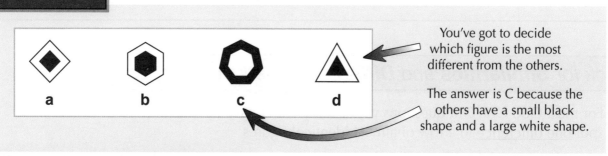

Odd One Out

You've got to decide which figure is the most different from the others.

The answer is C because the others have a small black shape and a large white shape.

Find the Figure Like the Others

1) Here's a <u>Find the Figure Like the Others</u> question:

You've got to decide which of the figures on the right is the most similar to the two figures on the left.

The answer is D. Every figure must have a circle and a five-pointed star.

2) <u>Find the Figure Like the Others</u> questions can have <u>two</u> figures on the left-hand side, or they can have <u>three</u> figures. You work out the answer for both in <u>exactly the same way</u>.

Writing Notes can help you learn how to do these questions

Here are some <u>useful tips</u> for <u>starting out</u> with these questions.

1) As you go through the <u>different parts</u> of each question to decide which ones will help you find the answer, <u>write down</u> the ones you've already looked at. This will stop you from looking at the same one <u>twice</u>. If you're <u>stuck</u> on a question, look back at the list of elements on page 4 and see if you're <u>missing</u> any from your list.

2) If you're <u>counting</u> something in each figure (e.g. the number of dots or the number of sides), <u>write down</u> how many you count for each one to help you <u>keep track</u> of the numbers.

These tips are useful when you're <u>learning</u> how to do the questions, but as you get <u>closer</u> to the <u>test</u>, you'll need to learn to keep track of these things <u>in your head</u>.

Odd One Out

For these questions, all you've got to do is spot the odd one out. Sounds pretty easy, but sometimes the pesky thing's hidden really well... Here are some tips to help you hunt it down.

Warm-Up Activity

1. Find another person to play this game with you. Each draw <u>five boxes</u> on a piece of paper and draw a <u>picture</u> inside <u>each box</u>. The pictures should all <u>look different</u>, but <u>four</u> should have something in <u>common</u> that the other one <u>doesn't</u> (e.g. four different cars and one lorry).

2. <u>Cut out</u> the boxes, <u>shuffle</u> them and <u>swap</u> them with the other person.

3. <u>Time</u> how long it takes each of you to find the picture that's <u>different</u> from the other four and say <u>why</u> it's the <u>odd one out</u>. The person who does this the <u>fastest wins</u>.

Look for **Similarities** and **Differences** between shapes

1) For most Odd One Out questions you usually won't have to spot <u>one difference</u> in a row of almost <u>identical</u> figures.

2) Instead, the options will probably look quite <u>different</u> — you'll need to spot something that <u>all but one</u> of the figures have <u>in common</u>. The option that <u>doesn't</u> have it is the <u>answer</u>.

<u>Tips and Tricks for Odd One Out questions</u>

Watch out for questions where two of the figures have something in common — remember that you're looking for <u>one</u> shape that's different from <u>all</u> the others.

Look at the figures to see if there are any **Obvious Differences**

Sometimes the answer to an Odd One Out question will be <u>quite simple</u>.

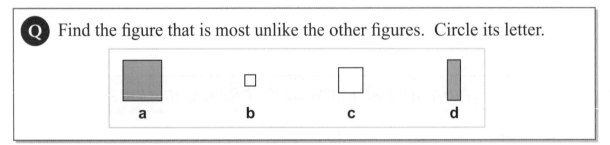

Q Find the figure that is most unlike the other figures. Circle its letter.

    a   b   c   d

Method 1 — Look for a simple answer

See if you can spot anything <u>straight away</u> — then quickly <u>check</u> your answer.

1) In this example, the odd one out must be <u>D</u> (a rectangle) because all the other figures are <u>squares</u>.

2) Look at the other elements to make sure you're right. All the shapes are <u>different sizes</u>, so you can't use size to spot the odd one out. Two figures are <u>white</u> and two are <u>grey</u> — this means that shading <u>isn't relevant</u>.

Question Types — Similarities and Differences

If the answer isn't **Obvious**, go through each **Element** one by one

Sometimes you <u>won't</u> be able to spot the odd one out <u>straight away</u>.

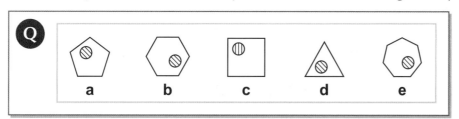

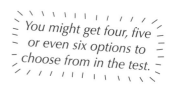

You might get four, five or even six options to choose from in the test.

Method 2 — Look at each element in turn

1) Think about the <u>different elements</u> that can come up (see p.4).

2) Check each one <u>in turn</u> until you find something that <u>four figures share</u>, and <u>one doesn't</u>.

---

1) <u>Large shapes</u> — they're <u>all different</u>, and there's nothing that four out of five have <u>in common</u>.

2) <u>Small shapes</u> — they're <u>all circles</u> that are the <u>same size</u>.

3) <u>Position</u> — the circles are in <u>different positions</u> in each white shape — position <u>doesn't help you</u> find the odd one out.

Don't spend too long on this method. If you're stuck, go on to the method below.

4) <u>Shading</u> — the large shapes are <u>all shaded the same</u>. <u>All</u> the small circles are <u>hatched</u>, but only four have the <u>same direction</u> of hatching. C has <u>vertical hatching</u> — the others all have hatching going <u>diagonally down to the right</u>, so the answer is <u>C</u>.

Sometimes you'll have to think about **More Than One Element**

In some questions you can only spot the odd one out by looking at a <u>combination</u> of different elements.

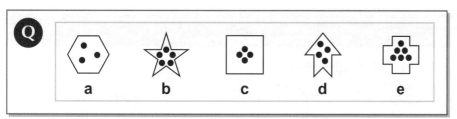

In this example, you could look at the <u>number of sides</u> the shapes have, the <u>number</u> of <u>dots</u>, the <u>size</u> of the shapes and the <u>symmetry</u> of the shapes without finding the answer. You need to try the <u>next method</u>:

Method 3 — Look at more than one element at a time

Look at how the elements <u>work together</u> — try to find <u>links</u> between them.

---

1) <u>Count the sides</u> of the white shapes — A has 6, B has 10, C has 4, D has 8, and E has 12. They all have <u>different numbers of sides</u> and they are all <u>even</u>, so you need to look at <u>something else</u>.

2) <u>Count</u> the number of <u>black dots</u> — A has 3, B has 5, C has 4, D has 4, and E has 6. You need to find something that <u>four figures</u> have in <u>common</u>, so this <u>doesn't help</u> either.

3) <u>Compare</u> these numbers — A has 6 sides and 3 dots, B has 10 sides and 5 dots, C has 4 sides and 4 dots, D has 8 sides and 4 dots, and E has 12 sides and 6 dots.

4) This shows that the <u>white shapes</u> in A, B, D and E have <u>twice</u> the number of <u>sides</u> as the number of <u>black dots</u>. C has the <u>same</u> number of sides as black dots, so it's the <u>odd one out</u>.

Question Types — Similarities and Differences

Sometimes the answer is *Simpler* than it *Looks*

If you can't find the answer after looking at <u>all the elements</u> in each figure and at different <u>combinations</u> of elements, try looking at the <u>simple</u> things again — some questions are <u>simpler</u> than they <u>look</u>.

> **Q** Find the figure that is most unlike the other figures. Circle its letter.
>
>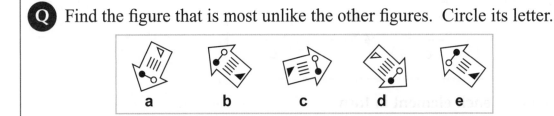
>
> a   b   c   d   e

Go through the elements again, to see if you've <u>missed anything</u>:

1) <u>Number of lines</u> — two figures have <u>five lines</u> and three figures have <u>four lines</u>.

2) <u>Shading of triangle</u> — two figures have <u>white triangles</u> and three have <u>black triangles</u>.

3) <u>Rotation of triangle</u> — all of the triangles <u>rotate with the arrow</u>. None of them are reflected.

4) <u>Shading of circles</u> — every figure has <u>one</u> black circle and <u>one</u> white circle.

5) <u>Position of circles</u> — in A, C, D and E, the black circle is on the <u>right</u> of the shape when the arrow is <u>pointing up</u>. In B it's on the <u>left</u> of the shape. This means that <u>B</u> must be the odd one out.

>
>
> ### Tips and Tricks for Odd One Out questions
>
> When the figures all look similar but are rotated differently, it might help to turn the page so you can look at them all the same way up.

Practice Questions

Which figure is the odd one out? Circle the right letter.

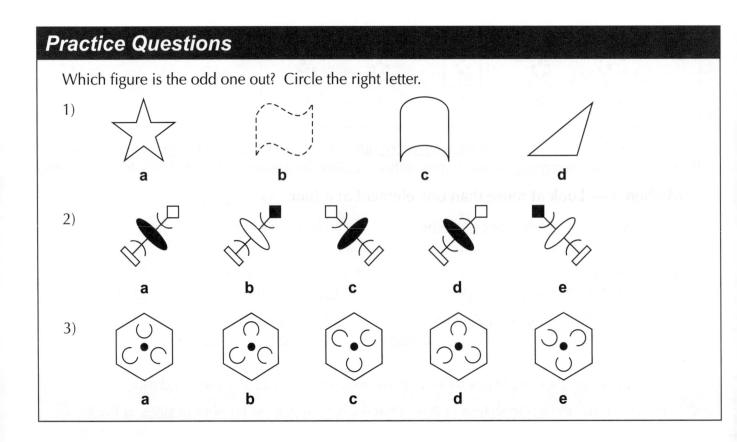

Find the Figure Like the Others

These questions are a bit like Odd One Out questions — you'll still be spotting similarities and differences — so the skills you practised in the last section will come in handy.

Warm-Up Activity

1. Find another person to play this game with you. <u>Cut</u> a piece of <u>card</u> into <u>18 squares</u>.

2. Draw each of these shapes on a different square: a <u>large red triangle</u>, a <u>large blue triangle</u>, a <u>large yellow triangle</u>, a <u>small red triangle</u>, a <u>small blue triangle</u>, a <u>small yellow triangle</u>. On the next 12 squares, do the <u>same</u>, but with <u>circles</u> and then <u>rectangles</u>.

3. <u>Shuffle</u> the squares and put them onto a table, <u>face down</u>. Take it in turns to turn over two squares. If they have <u>two things in common</u> (e.g. they're both small and red) you can <u>keep them</u>. If they don't, turn them back over and the other person takes their turn.

4. The <u>winner</u> is the person with the <u>most cards</u> when you can't make any more pairs.

The *Answer* has something *In Common* with the *Example Figures*

1) For these questions, you need to find something that <u>all</u> the example figures on the left of the page have <u>in common</u>, which <u>only one</u> of the answer options has too. That option is the <u>answer</u>.

2) You might get questions with <u>two</u> or <u>three example figures</u>.
   You can use the <u>same method</u> to answer both types of question.

3) The answers might all <u>look quite different</u>. Remember that you're <u>not</u> trying to find the one that <u>looks</u> most like the examples — look for the <u>only one</u> with the right <u>elements in common</u> with them.

Sometimes you'll *Only* need to look at *One Element*

Look at the <u>most obvious</u> things first — they might give you the <u>answer</u>, or <u>narrow down</u> the options.

> **Q** Find the figure that is most like the two figures on the left. Circle its letter.
>
>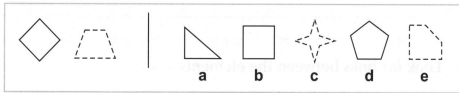
>
>   **a**   **b**   **c**   **d**   **e**

Method 1 — Look for obvious similarities

1) Find <u>one thing</u> that all of the example figures have in common.

2) If <u>only one</u> of the answer options also has that thing in common, then that must be the <u>answer</u>.

1) Both example figures are <u>white</u>, but all the options are also <u>white</u>, so that doesn't help.
   Each example figure has a <u>different type of line</u>, so that's not something they have <u>in common</u>.

2) Both example figures have <u>four sides</u>. <u>Only one</u> of the options has four sides — the answer is <u>B</u>.

Question Types — Similarities and Differences

You might need to look at **A Few** elements **Separately**

Often the example figures will have a few elements in common, that may not be linked. Instead of looking for all the similarities at once, use the method below.

Q Find the figure that is most like the three figures on the left. Circle its letter.

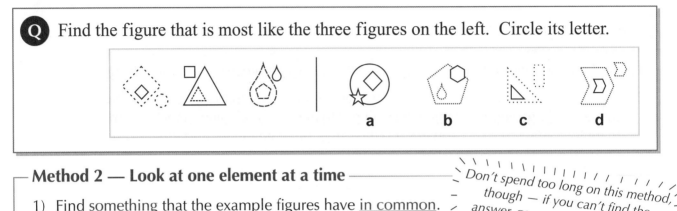

Method 2 — Look at one element at a time

1) Find something that the example figures have in common.
2) Rule out the answer options that don't have the same element.
3) Repeat these two steps until you're only left with one option — that's the answer.

Don't spend too long on this method, though — if you can't find the answer, go on to the next method.

1) **Type of line** — in each figure, the large shape has the same type of line as one of the small shapes. This rules out A (all of the shapes have the same type of line).

2) **Small shapes** — in each figure, only one of the small shapes must be the same as the big shape. This rules out D (all the shapes are the same) and B (they're all different). The answer is C.

The similarity could be a **Link** between **Two Elements**

If it's not obvious what the examples have in common, look at how different elements are related.

Q

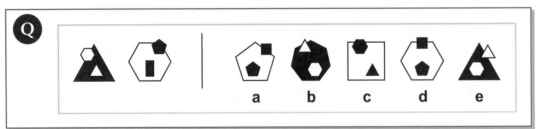

In this example, looking at the elements separately doesn't help you find the answer.

Method 3 — Look for links between the elements

Look at the different elements in the example figures to see if there are any links between them.

1) There aren't any links between the number of sides of the large shape and the two small shapes.

2) You could add up the number of sides of the two small shapes, but that doesn't help — the sides of the small shapes in both of the figures and all of the options add up to nine.

3) In the first example figure, the small shape at the top has six sides and the small shape below it has three. In the second figure, the small shape at the top has five sides and the small shape below it has four. The shape with the most sides is always on top.

4) Only option C has the shape with the most sides at the top — it must be the answer.

Question Types — Similarities and Differences

You *Might* need to *Look* for a *Pair* of *Rules* to find the *Answer*

1) For some questions, you might need to work out a <u>pair of rules</u>. The rules could be something like — 'If the shape is a square then it's white. If it's a circle then it's black'. The answer will be the <u>only option</u> which <u>follows</u> this rule.

2) <u>Only</u> look for <u>rules</u> if you <u>can't</u> solve the question any other way — rule questions are <u>very rare</u>.

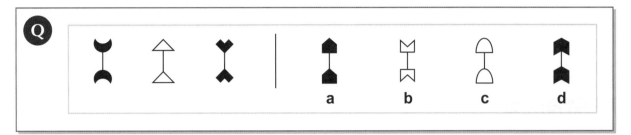

Method 4 — See if the example figures follow a pair of rules

1) Look for one example figure that has <u>two differences</u> from the other two example figures. In the middle example figure, the shapes at the end of the line are <u>white</u>, and have the <u>same rotation</u>, and in the others the shapes are black and are 180 degree rotations of each other.

2) Try to make a <u>pair of rules</u> out of these two differences. The rules in the example could be — 'If the shapes are <u>white</u>, then they have the <u>same rotation</u>. If they're <u>black</u> then they're <u>180 degree rotations</u> of each other.'

Odd One Out questions can have rules too, e.g. if the circle is inside the shape it's white, and if it's outside it's black. The odd one out breaks the rule (the circle might be white and outside).

3) If <u>only one</u> of the answer options follows this pair of rules, then that's the <u>answer</u>. The <u>only answer option</u> to follow this rule is <u>C</u>, so this must be the answer.

Practice Questions

Which figure is most like the two figures on the left? Circle the right letter.

1)

     a   **b**   **c**   **d**

Which figure is most like the three figures on the left? Circle the right letter.

2)

     a   **b**   **c**   **d**   **e**

3)

     a   **b**   **c**   **d**   **e**

Pairs, Series and Grids

These pages are about Complete the Pair, Complete the Series and Complete the Grid questions. Don't get your snap cards out yet, though — Complete the Pair isn't quite that fun...

You'll need to spot **How Figures Change**

1) These questions are all about spotting <u>changes</u> between figures.

2) Once you've spotted the change, you'll have to change <u>another</u> figure in the <u>same way</u>.

3) There are <u>three</u> main types of question in this section:

Complete the Pair

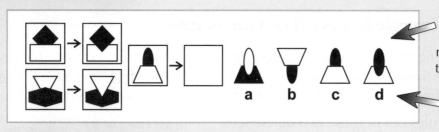

You've got to work out how the first two figures change to make the second figures. Then you need to make the same change to the third figure to find the answer.

The answer is D because the top shape moves from the back to the front.

Complete the Series

You've got to decide which of the figures on the right fills the gap in the series.

The answer is D because the arrow rotates 90 degrees clockwise in each square and the shading alternates.

Complete the Grid

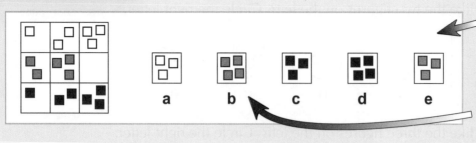

You've got to decide which of the figures on the right fills the gap in the grid.

The answer is B. The number of squares increases by one along each row, and all the squares in a row are the same colour.

Drawing the **Missing Figure** or **Writing Notes** can help you get started

These questions can be tricky at first, so here are some <u>tips</u> to help you <u>improve</u>:

1) Try <u>drawing</u> what you think should go in the <u>gap</u> in the series or grid, or what you think the <u>missing half</u> of the pair should look like. This'll help you to <u>imagine</u> what the answer should be.

2) You could also <u>write down</u> each <u>change</u> that you spot between the figures to <u>keep track</u> of them.

When you're more <u>confident</u> about these questions, and you're getting <u>close</u> to the <u>test</u>, you'll need to keep track of the changes and work out what the answer looks like <u>in your head</u>.

Complete the Pair

In these questions, you've got to be able to spot how figures change to make other figures. There might be a few changes to notice, but don't worry — just look at them one at a time.

Warm-Up Activity

1. Find another person to play this game with. <u>Each of you</u> should <u>draw two boxes</u> on a piece of paper. Inside the <u>first box</u>, draw a <u>picture</u> (or a collection of shapes) and <u>colour</u> it in. In the <u>second box</u>, draw the <u>same picture</u>, but <u>change four things</u> about it.

2. <u>Swap</u> pictures, and take it in <u>turns</u> to spot the <u>four differences</u> between the two pictures and describe them to your partner. <u>Time</u> how long it takes each of you — the <u>winner</u> is whoever does it the <u>fastest</u>.

Work out how the **First** figures **Turn Into** the **Second** figures

1) For Complete the Pair questions you'll be given two <u>pairs of figures</u>. You've got to work out which <u>element</u>, or <u>combination</u> of elements, changes in the first figures to <u>make</u> the <u>second</u> figures. Then you've got to change another figure <u>in exactly the same way</u> to get the answer.

2) The first two pairs of figures might <u>look very different</u> from the third figure and the options. Remember that you're <u>not</u> looking for the option that's <u>most similar</u> to the other two pairs.

You might only need to spot **One Change**

In easier Complete the Pair questions, only <u>one thing</u> will <u>change</u> between the first and second figures.

Q Look at how the first two figures are changed, and then work out which option would look like the third figure if you changed it in the same way.

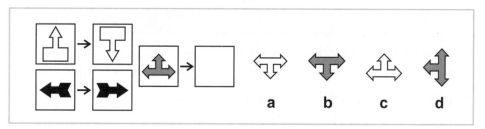

Method 1 — Look at the elements that change

1) First work out <u>what happens</u> to the first figures to <u>make the second figures</u>.

2) Then <u>do the same thing</u> to the third figure to find the answer.

1) In this example, the first figures are <u>rotated 180 degrees</u> to give the second figures.

2) If you <u>rotate the third figure</u> 180 degrees you get the answer — <u>option B</u>.

Question Types — Pairs, Series and Grids

For some questions you'll have to spot **More Than One Change**

In harder Complete the Pair questions, <u>more than one thing</u> will change between each pair.

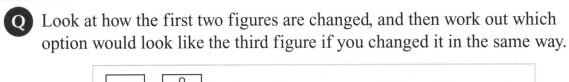

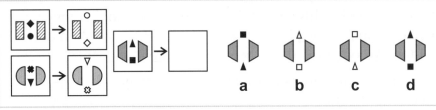

Method 2 — Narrow down the options

If <u>more than one thing</u> changes, use each change to <u>rule out</u> some possible answers.

---

1) <u>Small shapes</u> — the small shape at the <u>top</u> of the first figure in each pair moves to the <u>bottom</u> in the second figure, and the small shape at the bottom moves to the <u>top</u>. This means that the <u>answer</u> must have a <u>square</u> at the top and a <u>triangle</u> at the bottom. This <u>rules out</u> B and D.

2) <u>Shading</u> — the small shapes change from <u>black</u> to <u>white</u>. This <u>rules out</u> A — the <u>answer</u> is <u>C</u>.

The two **Halves** of each pair might **Look** very **Different**

Sometimes there will be a <u>big change</u> between the <u>first figure</u> and the <u>second figure</u> of the pair.

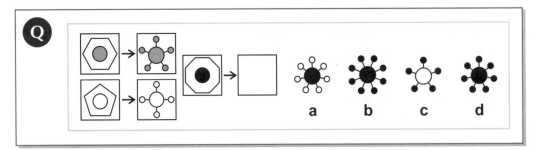

1) <u>Shading</u> — all the circles in the second figures have the <u>same shading</u> as the <u>circle</u> in the first figures. This means that the answer must have only <u>black circles</u>, which rules out A and C.

2) <u>Number of small circles</u> — in both of the second figures there is <u>one less</u> small circle than the <u>number of sides</u> that each white shape has. The white shape in the third figure has <u>eight</u> sides, so the answer must have <u>seven</u> small circles — the answer is <u>D</u>.

If the two figures in the first pair look very different, it's often a good idea to try counting things.

Tips and Tricks for the Test

If you're allowed to write on the test paper, put a line through the options you've ruled out. If you're not allowed, try putting one finger under every option, and then taking away your fingers as you rule them out. You'll end up pointing at the right answer.

Some questions might look **Very Different**

Sometimes questions might look <u>completely different</u> — you can solve them in the <u>same way</u> though.

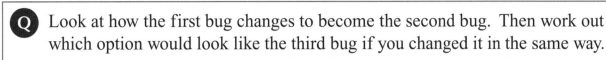

Q Look at how the first bug changes to become the second bug. Then work out which option would look like the third bug if you changed it in the same way.

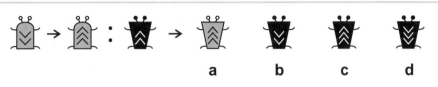

1) <u>Shading</u> — the bug's <u>body</u> and <u>antennae</u> don't change colour, which rules out option <u>A</u>.

2) <u>Number of lines</u> — one extra <u>v-shaped line</u> is <u>added</u> to the bug's body.
   This means that the answer must have <u>three v-shaped lines</u>, which rules out option <u>B</u>.

3) <u>Rotation</u> — the <u>v-shaped lines</u> on the bug's body <u>rotate 180 degrees</u>.
   This rules out option <u>C</u>, so the answer must be <u>D</u>.

Tips and Tricks for Complete the Pair questions

It's easy to confuse 'Complete the Pair' questions with a 'Find the Figure Like the Others' question (p.33-35). In this example, A is more similar to the first pair — it's there to confuse you. Remember what type of question you're answering.

Practice Questions

Look at how the first two figures have been changed. Which option on the right would look like the third figure if you changed it in the same way? Circle the right letter.

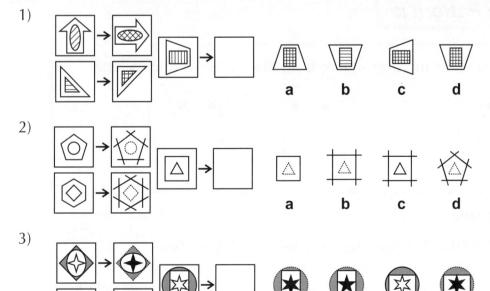

1)

    a   b   c   d

2)

    a   b   c   d

3)

    a   b   c   d

Complete the Series

For Complete the Series questions you've got to find the figure that completes a series.
You'd never have guessed. These questions are all about sequences and patterns.

Warm-Up Activity

1. Find another person to play this game with you. <u>Each of you</u> should draw a <u>line</u> of <u>four boxes</u> on a piece of paper. Inside the boxes, draw a <u>sequence</u> of <u>pictures</u> of things that happen in <u>order</u> — it could be getting up in the morning, doing the washing-up, etc.

2. <u>Cut up</u> the lines of boxes, <u>shuffle</u> them and then <u>swap</u> them over. <u>Time</u> how long it takes to put the pictures back in the <u>right order</u>. The person with the <u>shortest time wins</u>.

You have to find the **Missing Figure** in a **Series**

In Complete the Series questions, you'll be given a set of <u>four or five figures in order</u>, with one figure <u>missing</u>. You've got to choose the option that <u>fills the gap</u>.

There are **Different Kinds** of Series

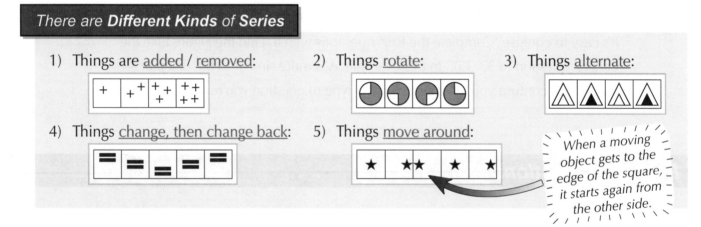

1) Things are <u>added</u> / <u>removed</u>:

2) Things <u>rotate</u>:

3) Things <u>alternate</u>:

4) Things <u>change, then change back</u>:

5) Things <u>move around</u>:

When a moving object gets to the edge of the square, it starts again from the other side.

Work Out what the **Pattern** is

Q Find the figure that is the missing square from the series. Circle its letter.

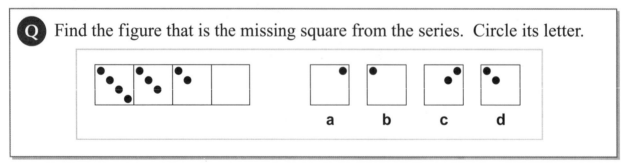

a   b   c   d

Method 1 — Find the rule

Look at any <u>elements that change</u> in the sequence, and work out the <u>rule</u>.

The <u>only element</u> that changes in this series is the <u>number of circles</u> — the bottom right-hand circle is <u>taken away</u> in each series square. The circles that are left stay in the <u>same corner</u> of the series square. This means that the answer must be <u>B</u> because it has <u>one</u> circle in the <u>top left-hand corner</u>.

Question Types — Pairs, Series and Grids

You might have to find **More Than One Pattern**

Some questions have <u>more than one element</u> that changes. Each change could follow a <u>different rule</u>. Look at <u>each element separately</u> to see <u>if</u> it changes, and <u>how</u> it changes.

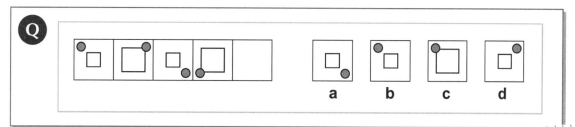

There are <u>two elements that change</u> in this series.

1) <u>Size of shape</u> — the size of the squares <u>alternates</u> between small and big. The fifth figure must have a <u>small square</u>, which rules out C.

2) <u>Position</u> — the circle <u>moves</u> around the <u>corners</u> of the series squares in a <u>clockwise</u> direction. This means that the fifth figure will have a circle in the <u>top left-hand corner</u>, so the answer is <u>B</u>.

> *Complete the Series questions can have a series with four or five squares.*

It **Won't Always** be the **Last Square** that's missing

1) <u>Any</u> of the figures in the series could be <u>missing</u>. If the <u>first</u> figure is missing, you might have to work <u>backwards</u> from the <u>end</u> of the series to the <u>beginning</u> to find the answer.

2) If one of the <u>middle</u> figures is missing, look at the figures on <u>either side</u> of the missing square for clues.

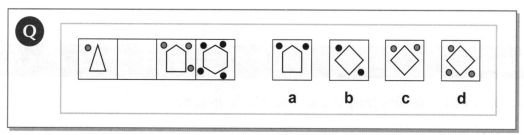

── **Method 2 — Look at the figures before and after the missing square** ──

Look at each element that <u>changes</u> in the series:

1) <u>Shape</u> — counting the <u>number of sides</u> of the white shapes gives the sequence: 3, ?, 5, 6. The sequence must be an <u>adding sequence</u> which goes: 3, <u>4</u>, 5, 6 — the missing shape must have <u>4 sides</u>. This rules out A.

2) <u>Number of circles</u> — counting the <u>number of circles</u> gives the sequence: 1, ?, 3, 4 — it <u>goes up by one</u> in each square. The missing square must have <u>two circles</u> — this rules out D.

3) <u>Colour of circles</u> — looking at the three figures in the sequence tells you that the colour of the circles <u>alternates</u> between black and grey. The first figure has a <u>grey circle</u>, so the answer must have <u>black circles</u>. This rules out C, so the answer must be <u>B</u>.

Some sequences can look very **Strange**

Sometimes looking at the <u>whole sequence</u> doesn't help — try <u>splitting it</u> into <u>two halves</u>.

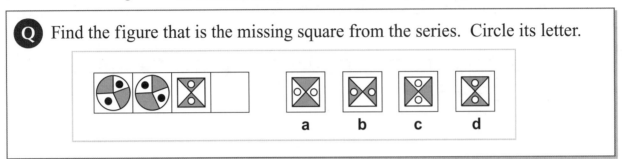

Q Find the figure that is the missing square from the series. Circle its letter.

a   b   c   d

In this example you can see what <u>changes</u> between the <u>first</u> and <u>second</u> squares, but the figure in the <u>third square</u> looks <u>very different</u>. You need to try the next method.

┌─ **Method 3 — Only look at the first two squares** ──────────

1) Look at what <u>changes</u> between the first square and the second square.

2) Work out what the <u>third square</u> would look like if it was changed in the <u>same way</u>.

1) <u>Shading</u> — the <u>four sections</u> of the circle in the first figure <u>swap</u> <u>shadings</u> in the second figure. This means the missing figure must have the <u>opposite shading</u> to the third figure (the sections on the right and the left must be grey). This <u>rules out A and D</u>.

2) <u>Position of dots</u> — the dots in the first two figures are always in the <u>white parts</u> of the circle. In the third figure, the dots are in the <u>grey parts</u> of the shape. This means that the dots in the <u>missing figure</u> must <u>also</u> be in the grey parts of the shape. This <u>rules out C</u>, so the answer must be <u>B</u>.

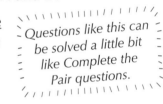

Questions like this can be solved a little bit like Complete the Pair questions.

Practice Questions

Find the figure that is the missing square from the series. Circle its letter.

1)

a   b   c   d

2)

a   b   c   d

3)

a   b   c   d

Complete the Grid

So the bad news is you've still got one more question type to get your head around in this section. The good news is that it's time for Complete the Grid, and everyone loves a grid.

Warm-Up Activity

1. Find another person to play this game with you. <u>Each draw</u> a <u>grid three squares high</u> and <u>three squares wide</u> on a piece of paper. Draw a <u>picture</u> that <u>fills all</u> the <u>squares</u> of the grid.

2. <u>Cut up</u> the grid, <u>pick one</u> of the squares and keep it <u>separate</u> from the others.

3. Try to <u>rearrange</u> the <u>other person's squares</u> to make the <u>original picture</u> (with a gap where the missing square should go). When you've made the picture, <u>draw what you think</u> should <u>go</u> in the <u>missing square</u> on another piece of paper.

4. The <u>winner</u> is the person whose <u>drawing</u> is <u>closest</u> to what's on the <u>missing square</u>.

You have to find the **Missing Figure** in a **Grid**

1) For Complete the Grid questions, you'll get a grid made up of either <u>squares</u> or <u>hexagons</u>.

2) <u>One</u> of the squares or hexagons in the grid will be <u>blank</u>.

3) You've got to find the figure that <u>fills the blank space</u> in the grid.

Start by looking **Along** the **Rows** of a **Square Grid**

> *Rows go from side to side.*
> *Columns go up and down.*

The first thing you should do is look along a <u>complete row</u> to see what happens to <u>each element</u>.

> **Q** Find the figure that fills the missing square in the grid. Circle its letter.
>
>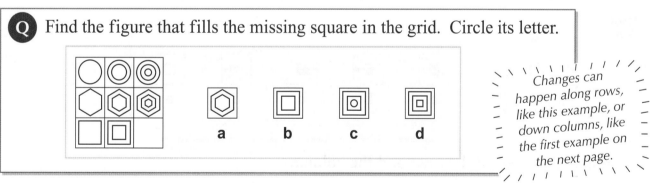
>
> *Changes can happen along rows, like this example, or down columns, like the first example on the next page.*

── **Method 1 — Find out what changes along each row** ──────

1) Look at a row with <u>no gaps</u> and work out <u>what elements change</u>.

2) To find the missing grid square, make the <u>same changes</u> to the row with the gap.

1) In this example, moving from <u>left to right</u> along the top row, a <u>smaller version</u> of the <u>circle</u> is added in each grid square.

2) To find the <u>missing square</u>, make the <u>same changes</u> to the bottom row of the grid. The bottom row has <u>squares</u> in it, so that rules out A and C. The third column must have <u>one more square</u> than the second column, so that rules out B. The answer must be <u>D</u>.

You might have to look for changes **Down a Column**

This example works <u>down the columns</u>, instead of <u>across the rows</u>. You can work out what goes in the missing grid square in exactly the <u>same way</u> — just spot what's <u>changed</u> in the columns without <u>gaps</u>.

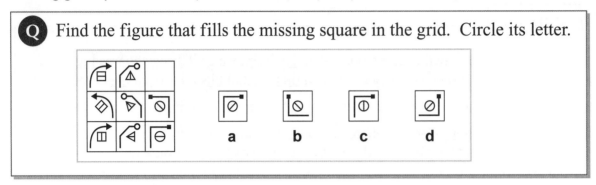

> **Q** Find the figure that fills the missing square in the grid. Circle its letter.

1) In this example, it's difficult to see any <u>connection</u> between the figures along each <u>row</u> — the figures are very <u>different</u>. To find the answer, you need to look down the <u>columns</u>.

2) Looking down the <u>left-hand column</u>, the arrow-style line <u>reflects across</u>. The square <u>rotates</u> 45 degrees anticlockwise going <u>down</u> the column.

3) The missing square is at the <u>top</u> of the grid, so you'll need to move <u>up</u> the <u>right-hand column</u> to find the answer — you'll have to make the changes <u>backwards</u>.

4) The arrow-style line in the middle right-hand grid square must <u>reflect across</u> to make the top right-hand grid square. The circle must <u>rotate</u> 45 degrees clockwise (because you're moving <u>up</u> the column instead of down it). The answer is <u>C</u>.

Grids can work **Horizontally** and **Vertically** at the **Same Time**

In some questions looking at <u>just</u> the columns or the rows <u>won't</u> give you the answer.

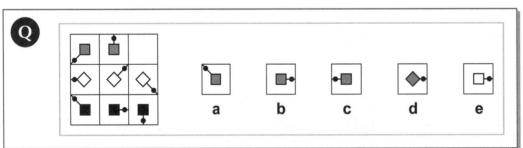

> **Q**

— **Method 2 — Look at the rows and the columns** —

Look at the <u>rows first</u>, and <u>rule out</u> as many options as you can. Then look at the <u>columns</u>.

1) In each <u>row</u>, all three small squares are <u>shaded</u> and <u>rotated</u> the same. This rules out D and E, but you're still left with <u>three possible answers</u>.

2) Going <u>down</u> each column, the black dot and the line rotate <u>45 degrees clockwise</u> around the grid square.

Treat each row and column as a 3-part series — spot patterns just like you would in a Complete the Series question.

3) The missing square is at the <u>top</u> of a column, so you've got to <u>work backwards</u> to find the answer — moving <u>anticlockwise</u> from the grid square below, the black dot must be in the middle on the right. The answer is <u>B</u>.

*The **Figures** in a **Square Grid** might make a **Pattern***

There are a few <u>different types</u> of pattern you need to look out for.

Different Kinds of Pattern

1) Two figures <u>alternate</u>.

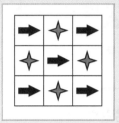

2) Each row <u>moves along</u>.

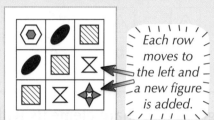

Each row moves to the left and a new figure is added.

3) The grid makes a <u>big picture</u>.

4) Each element <u>only appears once</u> in each <u>row</u>, once in each <u>column</u>, or once in each row <u>and</u> column.

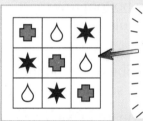

In this example, it's the shape that is different in each row and column, but it might be any element (e.g. line type, number or rotation).

5) Two different elements each <u>appear only once</u> in each row and column.

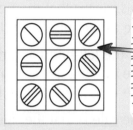

In this example, each number of straight lines (one, two and three) and each rotation of the lines both only appear once in each row and column.

Grids often have More Than One Pattern or Sequence to look for

The patterns above might be <u>combined</u> with other patterns or sequences.

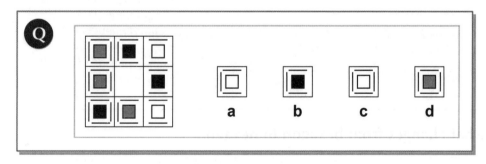

When the middle grid square of a row or column is missing, you'll have to look at the grid squares around it to find the answer.

1) In this example, along the <u>top and bottom rows</u> (from left to right) the <u>number of lines</u> changes from <u>four</u>, to <u>three</u> and then to <u>two</u>. The missing grid square is in the <u>middle</u> of a row, so it must have <u>three lines</u>. This rules out C and D.

2) Each <u>shading</u> of square (black, grey and white) <u>only appears once</u> in each <u>row</u>. This means the answer must be <u>white</u>. This rules out B, so the answer must be <u>A</u>.

In some questions, the contents of two of the grid squares are <u>added together</u> to make the third one.

Q Find the figure that fills the missing square in the grid. Circle its letter.

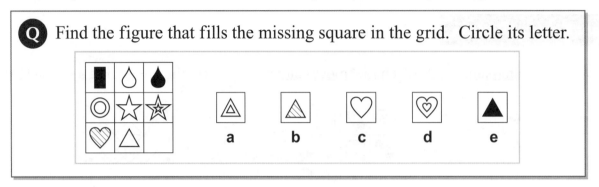

— **Method 3 — Look for figures that share elements with other figures** —

If you can't see a <u>sequence</u> or <u>pattern</u> in the grid, check the complete rows and columns for one figure that has elements from <u>the other two figures</u> in the same row or column.

1) In the <u>top two rows</u> of this example, the <u>middle</u> and <u>right-hand</u> grid squares both have the <u>same shape</u>. This means that the right-hand grid square in the <u>bottom row</u> must have the <u>same shape</u> as the <u>middle</u> grid square — a <u>triangle</u>. This rules out C and D.

2) In the top two rows, the <u>left-hand</u> and <u>right-hand</u> grid squares both have the <u>same shading</u>, so the missing grid square must have the same shading as the <u>bottom left-hand</u> grid square — it must be <u>hatched</u>. This rules out A and E, so the answer is <u>B</u>.

3) For this example, the <u>rule</u> is that the figure in the <u>right-hand</u> grid square in each <u>row</u> has the <u>same shape</u> as the <u>middle</u> grid square, and the <u>same shading</u> as the <u>left-hand</u> grid square.

Q Find the figure that fills the missing hexagon in the grid. Circle its letter.

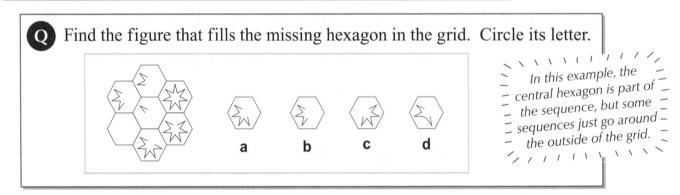

In this example, the central hexagon is part of the sequence, but some sequences just go around the outside of the grid.

— **Method 3 — Look at what changes from hexagon to hexagon** —

Look <u>around the outside</u> of the grid and try to work out what <u>changes</u> in each hexagon.

1) <u>Starting</u> from the <u>top</u> hexagon and going anticlockwise, each shape inside the hexagon has <u>one more point</u> than the one that comes before it.

2) There are three points before the missing hexagon and <u>five</u> points after it. The missing hexagon must have <u>four points</u> — this rules out B and D.

3) The points are added in an <u>anticlockwise</u> direction. This rules out C — the answer is <u>A</u>.

Question Types — Pairs, Series and Grids

The *Figures* in a *Hexagonal Grid* might make a *Pattern*

Here are a few of the patterns you'll need to recognise in <u>hexagonal grid</u> questions.

Different Kinds of *Pattern*

1) Identical shapes on <u>opposite</u> sides.

2) Shapes <u>reflect</u> across the <u>centre</u>.

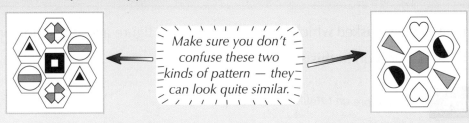

Make sure you don't confuse these two kinds of pattern — they can look quite similar.

3) The whole grid makes a <u>big picture</u>.

4) Two figures <u>alternate</u>.

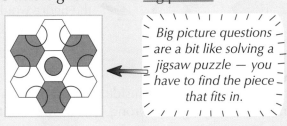

Big picture questions are a bit like solving a jigsaw puzzle — you have to find the piece that fits in.

Practice Questions

Which figure fills the missing space in the grid? Circle the right letter.

1)

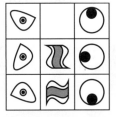

a   b   c   d   e

2)

a   b   c   d   e

3)

a   b   c   d

Question Types — Pairs, Series and Grids

Rotation and Reflection

This section is about recognising when shapes have been rotated or reflected. These two transformations can sometimes be tricky to tell apart, so read on for some handy tips.

You'll need to **Imagine** what **Objects** look like **Rotated** or **Reflected**

1) You'll be shown a figure and asked which of the options is that figure after a <u>rotation</u> or <u>reflection</u>.

2) There are <u>two</u> types of question in this section.

Rotate the Figure   *For more on rotation see p.20-22.*

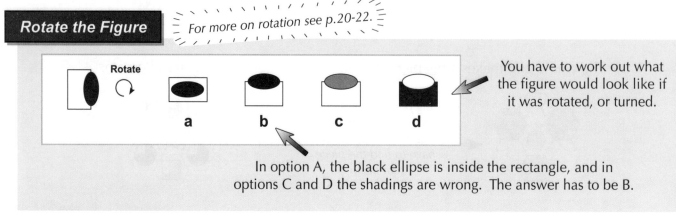

You have to work out what the figure would look like if it was rotated, or turned.

In option A, the black ellipse is inside the rectangle, and in options C and D the shadings are wrong. The answer has to be B.

Reflect the Figure   *For more on reflection see p.23-25.*

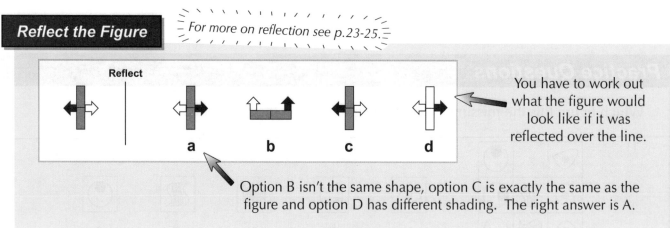

You have to work out what the figure would look like if it was reflected over the line.

Option B isn't the same shape, option C is exactly the same as the figure and option D has different shading. The right answer is A.

Investigating how objects **Rotate** and **Reflect** can be a big help

These questions can look a bit tricky at first, so here are some <u>tips</u> to get you <u>started</u>:

1) Try <u>drawing round</u> one of the figures above, using <u>tracing paper</u> if you have some. Then <u>turn</u> the paper around, to see what the figure looks like when it's been <u>rotated</u>.

2) If you're using tracing paper, you can also <u>flip</u> the paper over to see what the figure looks like when it's been <u>reflected</u>.

3) If you have a small <u>mirror</u>, you can put it beside a shape to see what its <u>reflection</u> looks like.

The <u>key</u> to rotation and reflection questions is <u>practice</u>. Practise using these tips at first until you can spot a rotated or reflected shape just by <u>looking at it</u>.

Rotate the Figure

In rotation questions, you'll be shown a shape and you have to work out which one of the options is a rotation of the same shape. Sounds easy enough, but it can get tricky.

Warm-Up Activity

1. Find another person to play this game with you. <u>Each of you</u> should <u>draw</u> five shapes down the side of a sheet of paper. (Try not to make them too <u>simple</u> or too <u>complicated</u>.) <u>Swap sheets</u> and try to draw the other person's shapes <u>upside down</u>.

2. <u>Cut out</u> the shapes and <u>turn</u> them around to compare them to the first drawings. The person who draws the <u>most rotations</u> correctly is the <u>winner</u>.

The **Answer** is the **Same** as the **Example Figure**

1) The <u>right answer</u> will be the option which is <u>exactly the same</u> as the example figure but rotated, or <u>turned</u>. All the other options <u>won't</u> be exactly the same.

2) If you <u>imagine rotating</u> the example figure, it will eventually look exactly the <u>same</u> as one of the options — that option is the <u>answer</u>.

Look at the **Options** to see if there is an **Obvious Answer**

Some questions might have quite <u>simple</u> shapes — see if you can spot an <u>obvious answer</u>.

Q Work out which option would look like the figure on the left if it was rotated.

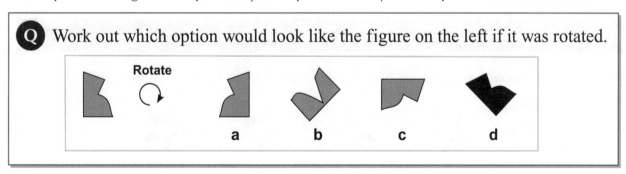

Method 1 — Look for a simple answer

Look at the <u>example figure</u> and see if you can spot an option <u>straight away</u> which might be the rotated shape — then quickly <u>check</u> your answer.

1) <u>C</u> looks like the figure <u>rotated 90 degrees clockwise</u>, so check that this is right.

2) A is a <u>reflection</u> of the figure on the left, so you can rule it out.

3) You can rule out B because it's <u>not the same shape</u>.

4) You can rule out D because it's a <u>different colour</u>.

Question Types — Rotation and Reflection

Sometimes you might need to **Narrow Down** the **Options**

The figure you need to rotate might be quite <u>complicated</u> — it might be <u>two or more</u> shapes together.

Q Work out which option would look like the figure on the left if it was rotated.

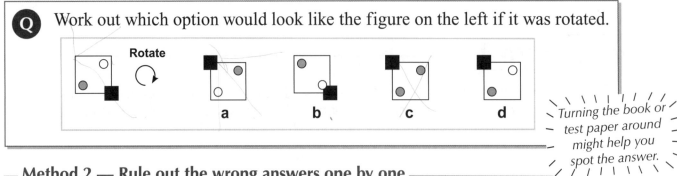

Turning the book or test paper around might help you spot the answer.

Method 2 — Rule out the wrong answers one by one

1) Look at each option <u>in turn</u> and try rotating it to see if it <u>matches up</u> with the example figure.

2) <u>Rule out</u> options which <u>don't match up</u> until you're left with one option that does.

1) In B, the black square is in the <u>wrong place</u>, so you can rule it out. The figure on the left has one grey dot and one white dot, but C has <u>two grey dots</u>, so you can rule it out.

2) You can rule out D because it's a <u>reflection</u> and then <u>rotation</u> of the example figure. (If you rotate the figure so that the <u>black square</u> is in the <u>right place</u>, the colours of the <u>dots</u> will be <u>wrong</u>.) That leaves <u>A</u> as the correct answer — it's been <u>rotated 180 degrees</u>.

Tips and Tricks for Rotate the Figure questions

First look for options which have the wrong shape or shading. Then, check any other options to see whether they have been <u>reflected</u> as well as rotated.

Practice Questions

Work out which option would look like the figure on the left if it was rotated.

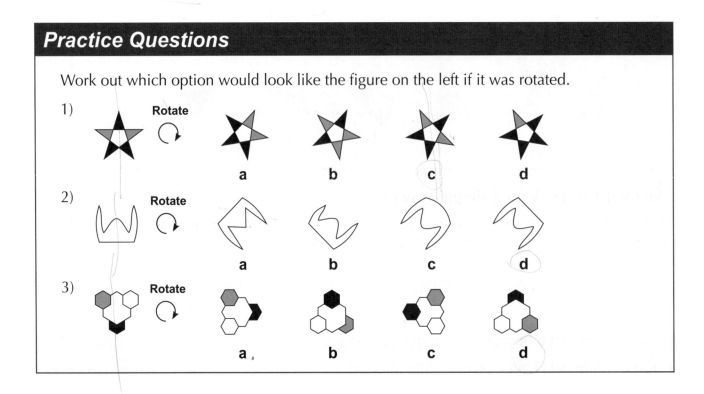

1)
2)
3)

Question Types — Rotation and Reflection

Reflect the Figure

The idea behind reflection questions is pretty simple — you've got to reflect a figure over a line. Unfortunately, some of the actual questions aren't as simple...

Warm-Up Activity

1. Find another person to play this game with you. Each of you should <u>draw a shape</u> on a separate piece of paper.

2. Swap shapes and have a <u>race</u> to see who can draw the <u>reflection</u> of the shape <u>fastest</u>. Then <u>check</u> with a <u>mirror</u> to see how <u>accurate</u> the reflected shapes are. The winner is the person who draws an <u>accurate reflection fastest</u>.

Find the **Option** that's a **Reflection** of the **Example Figure**

1) You'll be shown an <u>example figure</u> next to a line and four or five <u>options</u>.

2) You have to pick the option that's a <u>reflection</u> of the example figure over the line.

Try to spot an **Obvious Answer** first

The first thing to do is <u>imagine</u> what the example figure would look like if it was <u>reflected</u>.

Q Work out which option would look like the figure on the left if it was reflected over the line.

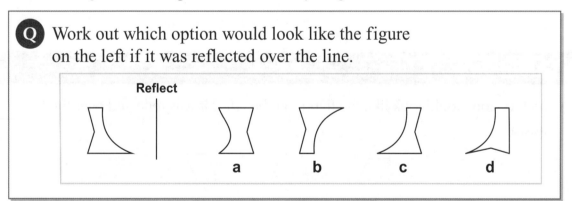

Method 1 — Imagine reflecting the example shape

1) Look for a <u>distinctive feature</u> on the example figure.

2) <u>Rule out</u> any options that <u>don't</u> have this feature.

3) Keep looking for <u>other features</u> and <u>ruling out options</u> which don't have them.

1) The right-hand side of the example image <u>curves down</u> from the top and out to the right. Its reflection will have the <u>opposite curve</u> on its left-hand side. The only options that are like this are C and D, so you can <u>rule out</u> A and B.

2) The <u>left-hand side</u> of the example figure has <u>two lines bent inwards</u>. The answer must have these lines on the <u>right-hand side</u>, so the correct answer must be <u>C</u>.

Sometimes the Figures can be quite Complicated

The figure can be more <u>complicated</u> than a simple shape — it might be <u>two or more</u> shapes together.

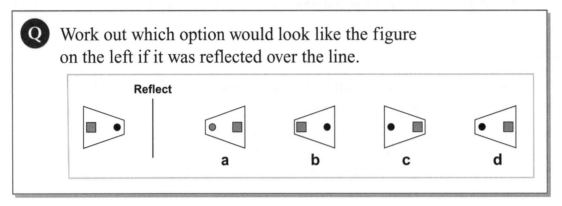

Q Work out which option would look like the figure on the left if it was reflected over the line.

Reflect

a   b   c   d

Method 2 — Look at each part of the figure separately

1) First look at the <u>largest</u> shape (or outline) and work out what its reflection should look like — <u>rule out</u> any answers that don't look like this.

2) Then look at any <u>smaller</u> shapes and rule out options where they're <u>not reflected correctly</u>.

1) In C, the <u>large white shape</u> has not been reflected, so you can rule it out.

2) Look at the <u>positions</u> of the dot and the square. Their positions have not been reflected in B, so you can rule it out.

3) In the figure on the left, the circle is <u>black</u>, but in A it is grey. This means you can <u>rule out A</u>, and the answer must be <u>D</u>.

Practice Questions

Work out which option would look like the figure on the left if it was reflected over the line.

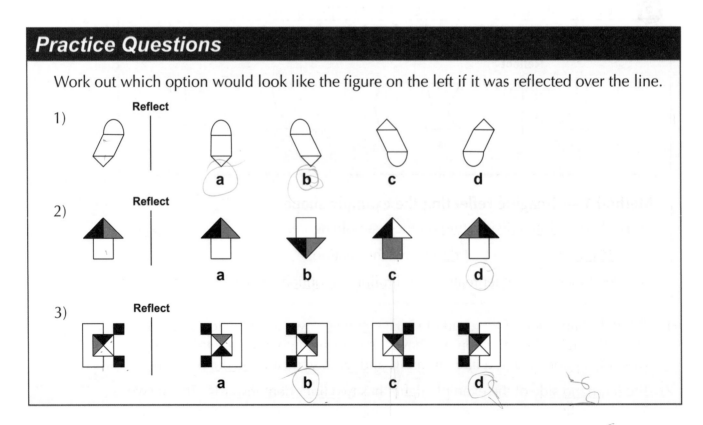

1) **Reflect**

      a   b   c   d

2) **Reflect**

      a   b   c   d

3) **Reflect**

      a   b   c   d

Question Types — Rotation and Reflection

3D Shapes

There's loads going on in this section, all involving 3D shapes. If you've got some building blocks handy, you could use them to make some of the figures — it might help you see what's going on.

You might need to **Rotate** 3D shapes

These questions are all about working out what 3D shapes would look like if they were <u>rotated</u>, <u>put together</u>, <u>taken apart</u> or <u>moved</u>.

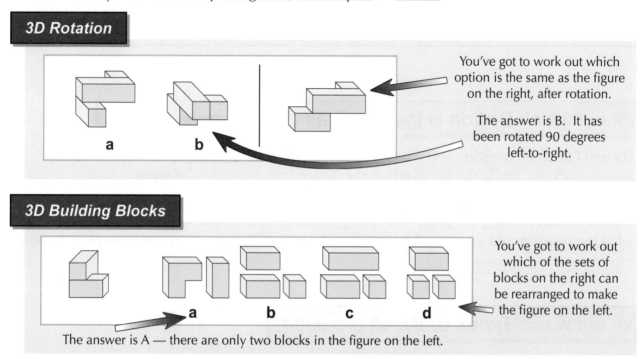

3D Rotation

a   b

You've got to work out which option is the same as the figure on the right, after rotation.

The answer is B. It has been rotated 90 degrees left-to-right.

3D Building Blocks

a   b   c   d

You've got to work out which of the sets of blocks on the right can be rearranged to make the figure on the left.

The answer is A — there are only two blocks in the figure on the left.

You might need to **Switch** between **2D** and **3D**

Here you'll need to imagine what <u>3D shapes</u> look like in <u>2D</u> and what <u>2D shapes</u> look like in <u>3D</u>.

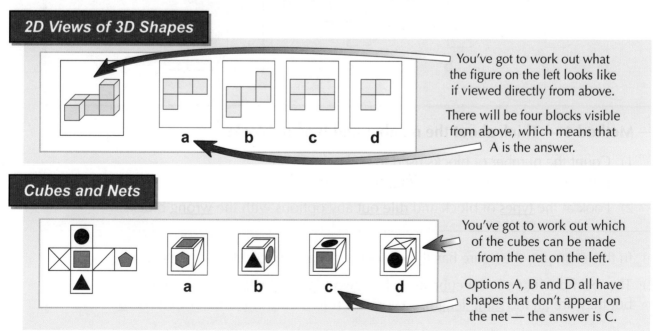

2D Views of 3D Shapes

a   b   c   d

You've got to work out what the figure on the left looks like if viewed directly from above.

There will be four blocks visible from above, which means that A is the answer.

Cubes and Nets

a   b   c   d

You've got to work out which of the cubes can be made from the net on the left.

Options A, B and D all have shapes that don't appear on the net — the answer is C.

3D Rotation

You've already had a go at rotating things in 2D — it's time to add another dimension. These questions are all about spotting 3D shapes after they've been rotated in 3D space.

Warm-Up Activity

Look around the room you're in and pick four <u>objects</u>, such as a mug or a lamp. Draw a quick <u>sketch</u> of them from where you're sitting. Then draw <u>another sketch</u> of what you think the <u>back</u> of the objects might look like. Look at the backs of the objects to see how <u>close</u> you were.

Work out which **Option** is the **Same** as the **Example Figure**

1) For a 3D Rotation question you'll be given several different <u>3D shapes</u> as <u>answer options</u>. You'll also be given another shape that is exactly the <u>same</u> as one of the answer options, except it has been <u>rotated</u>.

2) It can be rotated in <u>any direction</u> and by <u>any amount</u>. You have to try to <u>imagine</u> what the figure would look like if it was rotated, and <u>match</u> it to one of the answer options.

Work out which **Types of Block** are used

Sometimes you can find the answer just by looking at the <u>blocks</u> that make up the shape.

Q Work out which figure on the left has been rotated to make the new figure.

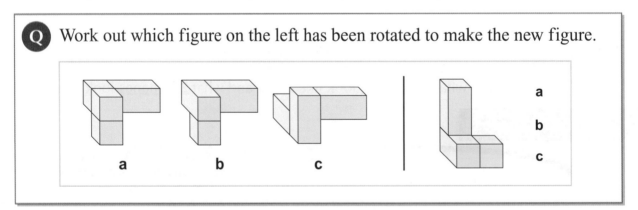

Method 1 — Think about the number and type of blocks

1) <u>Count</u> the number of blocks used to make the figure. <u>Rule out</u> any options with a <u>different</u> number of blocks.

2) Look at the <u>types</u> of block and <u>rule out</u> any options with the <u>wrong</u> blocks.

1) In this example, the figure has <u>three</u> blocks. A has <u>four</u> blocks, so you can <u>rule it out</u>.

2) The example figure has a <u>cube</u> as well as <u>two longer blocks</u>. C has three blocks, but they are <u>all</u> the <u>same length</u>, so you can rule it out. The answer must be <u>B</u>.

Look at the **Shape** of the **Figure**

Sometimes one part of a 3D shape is <u>easy to recognise</u>.

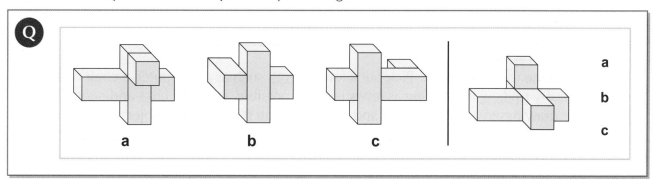

Q

a b c

Method 2 — Look for shapes that stand out

1) Look at <u>each</u> part of the figure and try to spot an <u>overall shape</u> that stands out. This could be something like an <u>L-shape</u>, an <u>S-shape</u> or a <u>cross</u>.

2) See if you can spot this shape in any of the <u>answer options</u>. Then <u>compare</u> the rest of the figure to the answer option to make sure that it <u>all</u> matches up.

---

1) The <u>base</u> of the figure on the right is a <u>cross</u> with one arm longer than the others. B has a cross, but all the arms are the <u>same length</u>, so you can <u>rule it out</u>.

2) In C, there is a <u>cube</u> attached to the <u>long arm</u> of the cross, instead of one of the <u>short</u> arms, so you can <u>rule it out</u>. The answer must be <u>A</u>.

Practice Questions

Work out which figure at the top has been rotated to make the new figure. Circle its letter.

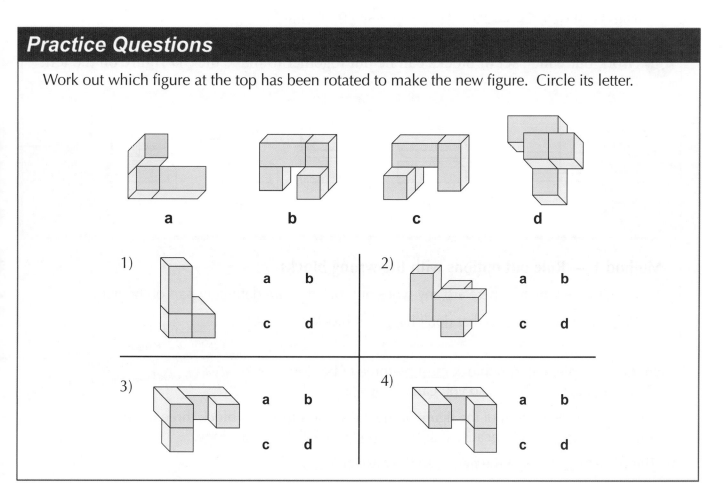

a   b   c   d

1)   a   b

          c   d

2)   a   b

          c   d

3)   a   b

          c   d

4)   a   b

          c   d

3D Building Blocks

These questions are all about imagining what groups of blocks would look like if you put them together to make a larger 3D shape. If you've got some building blocks, now's the time to use them.

Warm-Up Activity

Look around the room you're in. Pick out a few objects, such as a computer, a chair or a chest of drawers. Try to draw them using as few shapes as possible, such as cubes and cuboids. Show your drawings to another person and see if they can recognise the objects.

You have to **Build** the figure using **Blocks**

1) You'll be given a 3D figure that is made up of several blocks — usually between two and four. You'll also be given some sets of separate blocks.

2) You have to work out which set of blocks can be put together to make the 3D figure.

3) The blocks in the sets can be rotated by any amount and in any direction to make the figure. You'll have to imagine what the blocks would look like if they were rotated and combined.

Look for **Blocks** that are **Obvious**

In some questions, it is clear which blocks make up the figure.

Q Work out which set of blocks can be put together to make the 3D figure on the left.

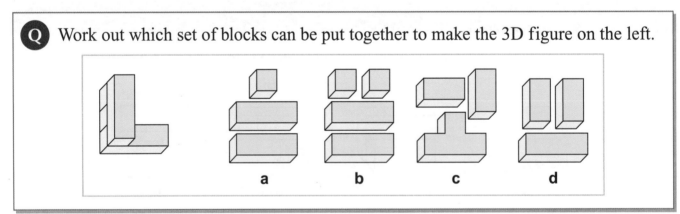

a   b   c   d

Method 1 — Rule out options with the wrong blocks

1) Look to see whether there are any types of block that are definitely part of the figure.

2) Rule out all the options that don't have that block.

The front of the figure is a good place to start — it's usually easier to tell which blocks are being used.

1) In this example, the front block must be three cubes long. C doesn't have this block, so you can rule it out.

2) The block at the bottom of the figure at the back also must be a block three cubes long. This rules out D because it only has one block three cubes long.

3) There are two cubes in the figure, so the answer is B.

Parts of some blocks could be **Hidden**

If part of the figure is <u>hidden</u> then it's not always easy to tell what blocks make up the figure.

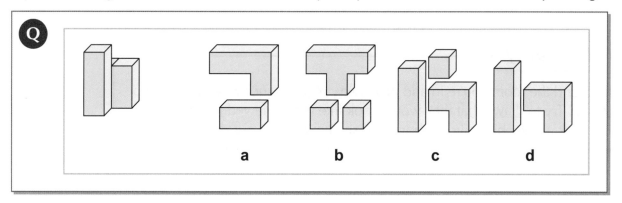

In this example, you can't tell <u>straight away</u> what the <u>front-left</u> block is — it could be a block <u>three cubes long</u>, an <u>L-shaped</u> block or a <u>T-shaped</u> block.

Method 2 — Think about what each block could be

1) Look at any blocks that you're <u>unsure</u> about and <u>work out</u> what they <u>could</u> be.

2) For <u>each possibility</u>, work out what the <u>other blocks</u> in the set would need to be.

1) If the front-left block was an <u>L-shape</u> three blocks high, A would be the <u>only</u> option. The block on the <u>right</u> of the figure could be the block at the <u>bottom</u> of set A, but there is still <u>another block</u> in the middle of the figure at the back. A <u>can't</u> be the answer.

2) The front-left block could also be a <u>T-shape</u>. However, B is the <u>only</u> option with a T-shape and <u>none</u> of the other blocks in B could be the block on the right of the figure. B can be ruled out.

3) This means that the front-left block <u>must</u> be a block <u>three cubes long</u>. There are at least <u>two other blocks</u> needed to make the figure. D <u>doesn't</u> have enough blocks — the answer is <u>C</u>.

Practice Questions

Work out which set of blocks can be put together to make the 3D figure on the left.

1)

2)

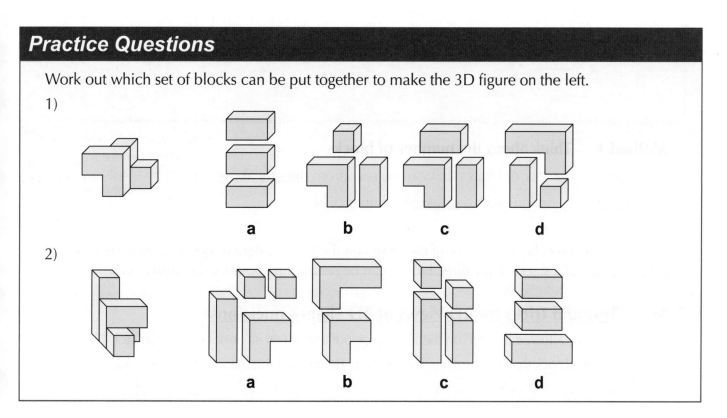

2D Views of 3D Shapes

Imagine looking at a cube from directly above. It will just look like a square on its own.
Now imagine you've got a group of cubes together and you're looking at them from above...

Warm-Up Activity

Look around the room you're in and pick a few <u>objects</u>, such as a table, a cup
or a chair. Try to <u>draw</u> what they would look like when viewed <u>from above</u>.
Have a look at the objects from above and see how <u>close</u> your drawings were.

You have to **Imagine** a **3D** shape in **2D**

1) You'll be given a <u>3D shape</u> made up of several cubes, and some <u>2D shapes</u> made up of squares.

2) You need to <u>imagine</u> what the 3D shape looks like when viewed <u>from directly above</u>.

3) Then you need to <u>choose</u> the option which <u>matches</u> this 2D view.

Work out how many **Blocks** you can see from **Above**

<u>Counting</u> the number of blocks that are <u>visible from above</u> is a good place to start.

Q Work out which option is a top-down 2D view of the 3D figure on the left.

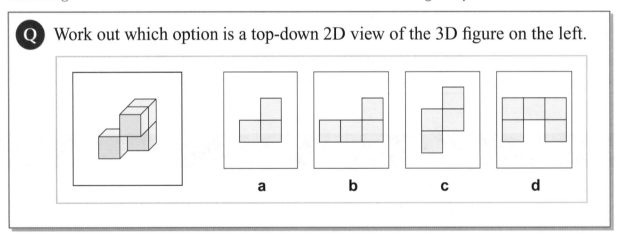

a   b   c   d

— **Method 1 — Think about the number of blocks** ———

1) <u>Count</u> the number of blocks that can be seen from <u>directly above</u>.

2) <u>Rule out</u> any options with a <u>different</u> number of blocks.

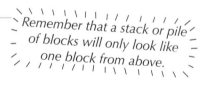
Remember that a stack or pile of blocks will only look like one block from above.

In this example, the cube at the back of the shape on the bottom-right <u>won't</u> be seen from above,
because it's part of a <u>stack</u>. Only <u>three</u> blocks can be seen from above — the answer is <u>A</u>.

Tips and Tricks for 2D Views of 3D Shapes questions

If you're allowed to write on the test paper, put a small cross or dot on the top face
of each block that can be seen from above. Then count the marks you have made.

Look at the **Positions** of the **Blocks**

Sometimes there will be a <u>gap</u> in the 3D shape that will make a <u>gap</u> in the 2D view.

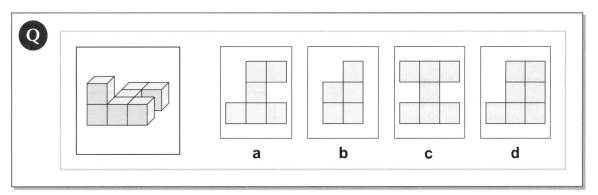

Method 2 — Look at the positions of the visible blocks

1) Count the blocks at the <u>front</u> of the figure and look for any <u>gaps</u> between them.

2) <u>Rule out</u> any options that don't look like this.

3) Do the same with the <u>other sides</u> of the figure until you find the right answer.

1) There are <u>three</u> blocks visible at the <u>front</u> of the figure — this <u>rules out</u> B.

2) On the <u>right-hand side</u>, there is a <u>gap</u> between the <u>front</u> and <u>back</u> blocks — this rules out D.

3) There are <u>two</u> blocks at the <u>back</u> of the figure — this rules out C. The answer is <u>A</u>.

Practice Questions

Work out which option is a top-down 2D view of the 3D figure on the left.

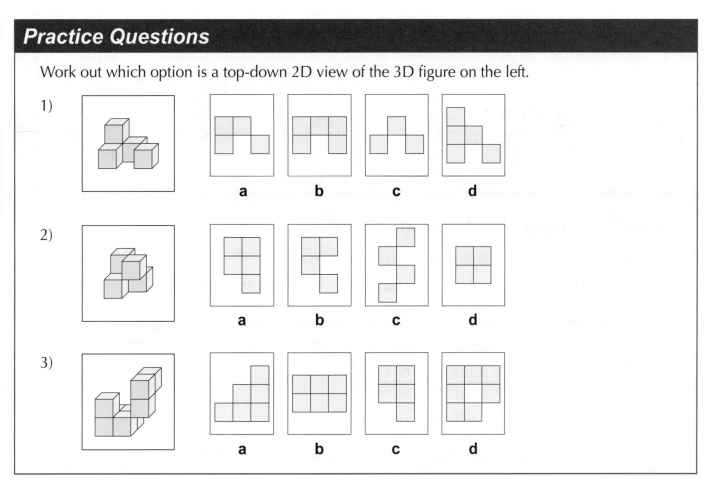

Cubes and Nets

This section's about turning 2D nets into 3D cubes. If you find these questions tricky, you could cut out some cube nets, draw the figures on them and fold them into cubes to see how they fit together.

Warm-Up Activity

Trace the net on the right and draw it on a new piece of paper. Cut out the net and draw a shape or design in pencil on each square. Fold it to make a cube and see how the shapes fit together.

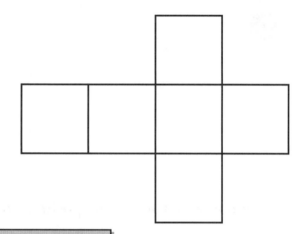

You have to work out which **Cube** matches the **Net**

1) For Cubes and Nets questions, you'll be given a net for a cube along with several cubes.

2) You'll have to work out which of the cubes can be made from the folded net.

Rule Out options that are **Wrong**

Sometimes you can rule out options without having to imagine folding the net.

> **Q** Work out which of the four cubes can be made from the net. Circle its letter.
>
>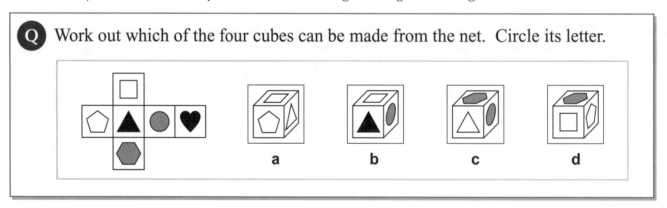
>
> a   b   c   d

Method 1 — Compare each cube with the net

1) Rule out options with shapes that aren't on the net.

2) Faces on opposite sides of the cube can't be seen at the same time — rule out any options where opposite faces appear together on the cube. You can tell when faces on the net will be opposite each other on the cube because they're separated by one other face.

1) In the example, you can rule out A and C because they both have a white triangle that isn't on the net.

2) The opposite faces of the cube in this example are the pentagon and the circle, the triangle and the heart, and the square and the hexagon. D has a square and a hexagon next to each other, so you can rule it out. The answer is <u>B</u>.

Some options might be **Harder** to **Rule Out**

Even if the shapes can all appear on the cube, they might be on the <u>wrong side</u> or <u>rotated incorrectly</u>.

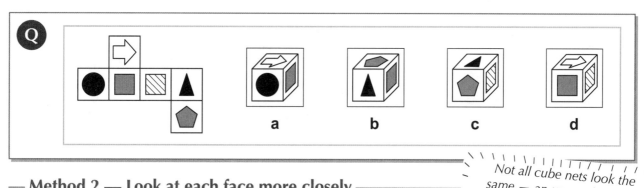

Method 2 — Look at each face more closely

1) Look at the direction a <u>shape</u>, <u>arrow</u> or <u>line</u> is <u>pointing</u> in.

2) <u>Check</u> where each <u>face</u> should be in <u>relation</u> to the <u>others</u>.

Not all cube nets look the same — an unusual one like this might come up in the test.

1) You can <u>rule out</u> B because the black triangle and the grey square must be on <u>opposite</u> sides of the cube, so they can't appear together.

2) In A, all the faces are in the <u>right place</u>, but the arrow <u>shouldn't</u> be pointing at the grey square — you can <u>rule it out</u>.

3) The cube faces in C can all <u>appear together</u>. However, if you folded the net so the triangle was at the top and the pentagon was at the front, the hatched square should be on the <u>left</u>, not the right. You can <u>rule out</u> C, so the answer must be <u>D</u>.

Practice Questions

Work out which of the four cubes can be made from the net. Circle its letter.

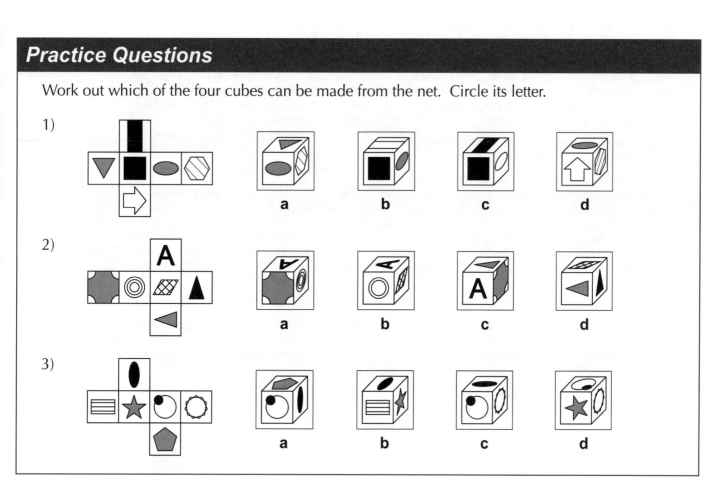

Answers

SPOTTING PATTERNS

PAGE 7 — SHAPES

Practice Questions

1.   D

All the other shapes have five sides.

(Counting the sides of each of the shapes shows you that D is the only shape that has a different number of sides from the rest, with four sides instead of five.)

2.   D

All figures must be triangles.

(Counting the sides of the example figures shows you that they both have three sides. D is the only figure that also has three sides.)

3.   A

The shape in the next series square always has one less side than the shape in the series square before it.

(Counting the sides of each of the shapes shows you that the number of sides of the shapes goes in the order: seven, six, five. This means that the next shape must have four sides. A is the only four-sided shape.)

PAGE 9 — COUNTING

Practice Questions

1.   B

All the other figures have the same number of lines crossing the outline of the shape as the number of black dots inside the shape.

(Keeping track of the number of small lines and dots in each figure shows you that there is a connection between the two types of object. B is the only figure which does not share this connection — it has two lines and three dots.)

2.   B

In all figures, the number of black shapes must be one less than the number of sides of the outer shape.

(Counting the number of sides of the large shape and the number of black shapes in the example figures shows you that there is a connection between the two — the first example has four sides and three black shapes, the second example has five sides and four black shapes. B is the only figure where the number of black shapes is one less than the number of sides of the large shape, with four sides and three black shapes.)

3.   B

An extra black dot turns grey in each series square.

(Keeping track of the number of black dots and grey dots in each figure shows you how many black and grey dots the next figure should have. The number of grey dots goes in the order: one, two, three. The next figure must have four grey dots. The number of black dots goes in the order: five, four, three. The next figure must have two black dots. B is the only figure which has four grey dots and two black dots.)

PAGE 11 — POINTING

Practice Questions

1.   D

In all other figures, the arrow is pointing away from a four-sided shape and towards a circle.

(If the arrows in all the figures don't share a common direction you should check whether the arrows all point towards or away from a common shape. D is the only figure in which the arrow points towards a four-sided shape and away from a circle.)

2.   A

The arrow switches between going clockwise and anticlockwise. The length of the arrow decreases in each series square.

(You can see that the arrow gets shorter in each square, so you don't have to work out how much smaller it is getting to realise that the missing square must have the shortest arrow. This means you are left with a choice between A and D. The arrow swaps between going clockwise and anticlockwise. The arrow in the third square is going clockwise, so you know that the arrow in the missing square must be going anticlockwise. This leaves you with A as the answer.)

3.   D

All arrowheads must point right.

(By looking at the example figures, you can see that they both point in the same direction. D is the only figure which also points right.)

PAGE 14 — SHADING AND LINE TYPES

1.   D

All shapes must be hatched and have a dashed outline.

(Looking at the example figures, you can see that they are both hatched. This leaves you with a choice between A and D. The two example figures also have the same sort of dashed outline. A has a solid outline, which leaves you with D as the answer.)

2.   A

An extra two squares turn black in each series square.

(The number of black squares goes in the order: two, four, six. The missing figure must have eight black squares. A is the only figure with eight black squares, so it must be the answer. You could also work out the answer by looking at the white squares, which go in the order: fourteen, twelve, ten. The missing figure must have eight white squares, which also gives you A.)

3.   E

All the other figures are made up of four lines.

(By counting the lines for each figure you can see that E has five lines, while the rest only have four. You could also look at the number of gaps in each figure's outline to work out the answer.)

PAGE 17 — POSITION

Warm-Up Activity
Tangram Square

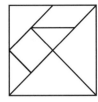

Practice Questions

1.   B

The heart moves round the shape one side at a time in an anticlockwise direction. The arrow moves up the middle of the hexagon.

(By working out the movement of both the small shapes, you know that the next square must have the arrow at the very top of the hexagon, and the heart on the right-hand side of the hexagon at the bottom. B is the only option that fits both of these descriptions.)

2.   C

In all other figures, the shapes are in the same positions — in C the circle and the raindrop have swapped places.

(Checking the position of each shape in turn will help you spot any differences.)

3.   A

In each series square, a shape is removed in a clockwise direction.

(Counting the shapes in each square shows you that there is one less shape each time, going in the order: six, five, four. The missing figure must have three shapes. This leaves you with a choice between A and C. Because the shapes are removed in a clockwise direction the cross should be the next shape to disappear. In C the star has been removed, which leaves you with A as the answer.)

PAGE 19 — ORDER

Practice Questions

1.   D

Working clockwise, the shapes in all the other figures go in the order: ellipse, star, trapezium.

(Picking the same small shape on the outline as a starting point and then counting round in the same direction for each of the figures will help you work out if the shapes are in an order. The order is the same for all the figures, apart from D, which has the order: ellipse, trapezium, star.)

2.   A

Each shape moves one place to the left in each series square.

(The shapes in all the examples have the same order: circle, square, hexagon (going from left to right). When the shape on the left-hand side can't move any further left, it appears again on the right-hand side in the next series square. A is the only figure where all the shapes are in the right order and the right positions: circle, square, hexagon (from left to right). Because there are only three shapes and three positions, it looks identical to the figure in the first square.)

PAGE 22 — ROTATION

Practice Questions

1.   A

The figure has been rotated 135 degrees clockwise. Options B and D are rotated reflections. Option C is the wrong shape.

(To help you see the rotation, take one part of the figure and rotate the page so that this one part faces the same way in each figure. If you rotate all the options so the longest side of the shape is on the bottom, you will notice that in B and D the cross shape is on the right instead of the left. They have been reflected. This leaves you with a choice between A and C. There is no cross shape in figure C, which leaves you with A as the answer.)

2.   A

The black quarter-circle rotates 45 degrees anticlockwise around the centre of each series square. The diamond rotates 90 degrees anticlockwise in each series square.

(To help you see the rotation of the quarter-circle, pick one of the straight edges of the quarter-circle and see how it has rotated in the next square. The quarter-circle in the missing square must be a 45 degree anticlockwise rotation of the quarter-circle in the third square, so it must be on the left-hand side of the square. This leaves you with a choice between A and D. Picking either the grey or the white half of the diamond and following it round will help you work out how the diamond is rotating. The next square must have the diamond rotated so that the grey half is on the right, which leaves you with A as the answer.)

3.   C

Ignoring the hatching, the right-hand shape in all figures must be a 90 degree clockwise rotation of the left-hand shape. The hatching in the right-hand shape must be a 45 degree anticlockwise rotation of the hatching in the left-hand shape.

(This question shows why you should always double check how the hatching of a shape changes. If you thought that both the shape and the hatching rotated 90 degrees together, you would get D as the answer. If you work out the rotation of the right-hand shape, you are left with a choice of C and D. C is the only option that has the correct hatching rotation. Rotating the page might help you work out how the shape and hatching should look in the right-hand shape.)

PAGE 25 — REFLECTION

Practice Questions

1.   B

In all other figures the bottom shape is a downwards reflection of the top shape.

(Imagining a horizontal line dividing each of the figures in half might make the reflection easier to see. The black shading of the bottom shape in figure B is the wrong way round for it to be a reflection — the bottom shape is actually a 180 degree rotation of the top shape.)

2.   C

In options A and B, the black circle is in the wrong place in relation to the arrow. Option D is a 180 degree rotation.

(In this question you have to imagine that there is a mirror along the 'reflect' line. The circle is at the top on the side closest to the mirror, so in the reflection the circle will also be at the top on the closest side (the left-hand side). This leaves you with a choice between B and C. The arrow is at the bottom, so in the reflection the arrow will also be at the bottom. This leaves you with C as the answer.)

3.   C

The shape rotates 90 degrees anticlockwise and moves to the next side of the series square in an anticlockwise direction. After rotation, the shape reflects back on itself over its longest side.

(This is quite a difficult question because the mirror line changes position in each square. To make it easier to see the mirror line you could rotate the page so that the shape is always at the bottom of each square.)

PAGE 28 — LAYERING

Practice Questions

1.   E

In all other figures, the hatched shape is a 90 degree clockwise rotation of the shape made by the overlap of the two white shapes.

(The hatched shape in figure E is not the same shape as the overlap of the two white shapes, no matter how it is rotated — it's actually the shape left when you take the overlap away from the triangle.)

2.   B

All figures must have a black shape at the front, and a white shape at the back.

(Looking at the example figures, they both have shapes layered in the same order from front to back: black, grey, white. A has both the white shape and the black shape at the front. C has a grey shape at the front and D has a grey shape at the back. This means that B is the only option that has the colours on the right layers.)

3.   D

Working from front to back, all other figures go in the order: pentagon, ellipse, arrow.

(You can check the order by picking the same shape to start with in all figures, and counting from that shape back. In D, the arrow and the ellipse have swapped places, giving the order: pentagon, arrow, ellipse.)

QUESTION TYPES

PAGE 32 — ODD ONE OUT

Practice Questions

1.   B

All of the other figures have a solid outline.

(The figures are all the same colour and all the shapes are different, so neither of these things help you find the odd one out. A and C are symmetrical, but B and D don't have any lines of symmetry, so symmetry doesn't help you either. They all have solid outlines except B, which has a dashed outline, so this must be the answer.)

2.   D

In all other figures, the ends of the curved lines point away from the ellipse. In D, they point towards the ellipse.

(All five of the figures are identical except for rotation, colour and the direction the curved lines point in. Figures A, C and D have the same colour scheme as each other. Figures B and E have the same colour scheme as each other, so colour doesn't help you find the odd one out. Figures A, B and D are rotated the same way, and figures C and E are rotated the other way, so rotation doesn't help you either. Only D has its curved lines pointing in a different direction from the other four, so that must be the odd one out.)

3.   A

In all other figures, two of the arcs have their gaps facing the black dot, and one has its gap facing the edge of the hexagon.

(All the figures are white hexagons with black dots in the centre, and they all have three arcs, so none of these things are helpful when you're looking for the odd one out. In figures A, B and D there's one arc at the top and two at the bottom. In figures C and E, there are two at the top and one at the bottom — this doesn't help you find the odd one out either. Only A has arcs pointing in a different direction to the rest, so this must be the answer.)

PAGE 35 — FIND THE FIGURE LIKE
THE OTHERS

Practice Questions

1.   C

All figures must have a small white shape inside a larger grey shape.

(The example figures both have two shapes, and one of the shapes is inside the other one. This leaves options B and C. In both the example shapes the inside shape is white. Figure B has a grey inside shape, which means the answer must be C.)

2.   D

*In all figures, the number of black dots must
be the same as the number of sides on the
shape with the smallest number of sides.*

*(The first example figure has three dots, one shape with
three sides and one with four sides. The second example
figure has five dots, one shape with five sides, and one with
six sides. The third has four dots, one shape with four sides,
and one with six sides. D is the only option that shares
the same connection as the example figures, with four
dots, one shape with four sides, and one with five sides.)*

3.   B

*In all figures, the arrow must go clockwise
around the circle. The beginning and the end
of the arrow must line up with the beginning
and the end of the black part of the circle.*

*(In all three of the example figures, the arrow goes clockwise
around the circle. Figures C and E have arrows going
anticlockwise and D has two arrowheads. This leaves options
A and B, so you've got to look back at the example figures to
see what else they've got in common. In all the example figures
the arrow lines up with the beginning and end of the black part
of the circle. The arrow in figure A doesn't line up with the
black part of the circle. This means that B is the answer.)*

PAGE 39 — COMPLETE THE PAIR

Practice Questions

1.   D

*The figure is rotated 90 degrees clockwise and
the hatching becomes cross-hatched.*

*(In the first pair, the ellipse and the arrow both rotate
90 degrees clockwise. The hatching inside the ellipse
changes from being hatched to cross-hatched. In the
second pair, the triangles both rotate 90 degrees
clockwise. The hatching inside the smaller triangle changes
from being hatched to cross-hatched. The same thing must
happen to the third pair — the rectangle and the trapezium
both rotate 90 degrees clockwise, so that the shortest
side of the trapezium is at the bottom. This rules out A
and C. The hatching inside the rectangle becomes
cross-hatched. This rules out B, so the answer is D.)*

2.   B

*The lines that form the sides of the large shape
get longer so they cross each other. The outline of
the small shape changes from solid to dotted.*

*(In the first pair, the lines that make up the pentagon's
sides get longer so they cross over. The small circle's
outline changes from solid to dotted. In the second pair,
the lines that make up the hexagon's sides get longer so
they cross over. The small diamond's outline changes from
solid to dotted. This means that in the third pair, the lines
that make up the square's sides get longer, which rules
out A and D. The small triangle's outline changes from
solid to dotted, which rules out C, so the answer is B.)*

3.   D

*The larger white shape rotates 90 degrees
and the outline of the grey shape changes from
solid to dotted. The star turns black.*

*(In the first pair, the ellipse rotates 90 degrees. The outline
of the diamond changes from solid to dotted and the
star turns black. In the second pair, the hexagon rotates
90 degrees. The outline of the circle changes from solid
to dotted and the star turns black. In the third pair, the
rectangle rotates 90 degrees, which rules out A and B.
The outline of the grey circle changes from solid to dotted,
which rules out C, which means the answer must be D.)*

PAGE 42 — COMPLETE THE SERIES

Practice Questions

1.   A

*In each series square, another section of the
pentagon becomes hatched in a clockwise direction.
The line between the old hatched section and the
new hatched section disappears. The hatching
rotates 90 degrees in each series square.*

*(Each large shape in the series is a pentagon, which rules
out B. The lines between the sections disappear
when the sections become hatched, which rules out D.
The hatching from the fourth square rotates 90
degrees, which rules out C, so the answer must be A.)*

2.   C

*In each series square, one black triangle
gets replaced by one white circle.*

*(Counting the number of each type of shape in the series
squares is a good place to start. The number of black
triangles goes down by one in each series square: four,
three, two. There must be one black triangle in the fourth
series square, which rules out B and D. The number of
white circles goes up by one in each series square: one, two,
three. There must be four white circles in the fourth series
square, which rules out A, so C must be the answer.)*

3.   B

*In each series square, the circle moves clockwise
around the four points of the star. The gap in
the star's outline moves one side clockwise.*

*(Working backwards along the series (from right to
left), you can see the circle and the gap in the star's
outline moving anticlockwise around the star. The next
position the circle will be in is on the left-hand point of
the star, which rules out A and C. The next position
the gap will be in is on the right-hand side of the top
point. This rules out D, so B must be the answer.)*

PAGE 47 — COMPLETE THE GRID

Practice Questions

1.   C

Working from top to bottom, the shape rotates
90 degrees anticlockwise in each grid square.

(The shapes in each column are all the same, which rules out
A, B and E. Working from bottom to top, the shape rotates
90 degrees clockwise in each column, so C is the answer.)

2.   E

Each pattern inside the squares only appears once in
each row and column. Along each row, the grid square
on the right contains both of the right-angled lines from
the left-hand grid square and the middle grid square.

(The only pattern which hasn't already appeared in the
bottom row and the middle column is the pattern made of
eight triangles, which leaves options C and E. Looking along
the first two rows, the right-hand grid square has two
right-angled lines and the other two squares only have one. The
two in the right-hand square are in the same positions as the
two in the left-hand and middle squares. On the bottom row,
the two lines are in the top right-hand and bottom left-hand
corners. The left-hand square has a right-angled line in the top
right, so the answer must have one in the bottom left-hand
corner. This rules out option C, so the answer must be E.)

3.   B

Going clockwise around the hexagonal grid, the shaded
corner of the triangle moves one corner clockwise. The
colour of the shading alternates between black and grey.

(The shading of the triangle changes position in each hexagon.
Starting from the top hexagon and going clockwise, the
shading is in the position: top, bottom-right, bottom-left.
The missing triangle should have the shading at the top of
the triangle, which rules out A and C. The shading alternates
between black and grey. On either side of the missing
hexagon, the shading is black, so the shading in the answer
must be grey. This rules out D, so B is the answer. You could
also find the answer by noticing that the figure is the same
in opposite hexagons, but with the shading changed.)

PAGE 50 — ROTATE THE FIGURE

Practice Questions

1.   C

The figure has been rotated 45 degrees clockwise.
The other figures are all shaded incorrectly.

(There are two grey points on the star, which rules
out B and D. The two grey points are not next to
each other, which rules out A. The answer is C.)

2.   D

The figure has been rotated 225 degrees
clockwise (or 135 degrees anticlockwise).
The other figures are all the wrong shape.

(The middle part of the figure should be a curve, which rules
out A. The two 'arms' on either side of the figure should be the
same length, which rules out B. There should be one straight
line in the figure, which rules out C, so the answer is D.)

3.   D

The figure has been rotated 180 degrees. A is a
rotated reflection. B and C are both layered incorrectly.

(The small grey and white hexagons should both be in
front of the large white hexagon, and the black hexagon
should be behind it. This rules out B and C. If A and D were
rotated so the black hexagon was at the bottom, the grey
hexagon should be on the left-hand side. This shows that
A is a rotated reflection, so the answer must be D.)

PAGE 52 — REFLECT THE FIGURE

Practice Questions

1.   B

Figure A is the wrong shape. C is a rotated
reflection. D is a 180 degree rotation.

(The semicircle is at the top of the figure, so in a
reflection across it will stay at the top of the figure,
which rules out C and D. The white parallelogram has
become a white rectangle in A, so B is the answer.)

2.   D

Figure A is identical to the figure on the left. B is
a reflected rotation. C has the wrong shading.

(In the figure, the grey triangle is closest to the
line of reflection, so the answer will also have the
grey triangle closest to the line of reflection.
This rules out A, B and C, so D is the answer.)

3.   B

Figures A and D have the wrong shading.
In C, the large white rectangle and the small
black squares have not been reflected.

(The large white rectangle is on the left-hand side of the figure
on the left, so the answer will have the white rectangle on the
right-hand side. This rules out C. The triangle at the top is
black, and will also be black in the reflection, which rules out
A. The triangle furthest from the line of reflection is grey,
so the answer will also have the grey triangle furthest from
the line of reflection, which rules out D, so the answer is B.)

PAGE 55 — 3D ROTATION

Practice Questions

1.   A

The figure has been rotated 90 degrees anticlockwise in
the plane of the page, then 180 degrees left-to-right.

(You could also look at the types of blocks to find the
answer. The figure in this question has one cube and
two blocks which are two cubes long. B, C and D all have
different sets of blocks, so A must be the answer.)

2.   D

The figure has been rotated 90 degrees
clockwise in the plane of the page. It has then
been rotated 180 degrees left-to-right.

(The figure in this question has two blocks two cubes long
that make an L-shape. There is a block attached to the
middle of the L-shape which could be one block two cubes
long, or a cube attached to another cube. D is the only option
which matches this shape, so it must be the answer.)

3.   B

The figure has been rotated 180 degrees in
the plane of the page. It has then been rotated
90 degrees towards you top-to-bottom.

(The figure in this question has a C-shape at the top.
This matches the shape of B and C, which rules out A and D.
The cube sticking out at the bottom of the figure is attached
to a block two cubes long, which rules out C, so B is the answer.)

4.   C

The figure has been rotated 180 degrees in
the plane of the page. It has then been rotated
90 degrees towards you top-to-bottom.

(The figure in this question has a C-shape at the
top, which rules out A and D. The cube sticking out
at the bottom of the figure is attached to another
cube, which rules out B, so C is the answer.)

PAGE 57 — 3D BUILDING BLOCKS

Practice Questions

1.   B

The block on the right of set B moves behind the
block on the left of the set. The block at the top of
set B moves to the right at the back of the figure.

(The block at the front of the figure must be a short
L-shaped block, which rules out A and D. The back of the
figure must be made of either three cubes, an L-shaped
block, or one cube and a block two cubes long. C doesn't
have any of those possibilities, so B is the answer.)

2.   A

One of the cubes at the top of set A moves in front
of the L-shaped block to become the front of the
figure on the left. The block on the left of set A
moves behind the L-shaped block and the other
cube moves to the right of this block to become
the back right-hand part of the figure.

(The front two blocks must be a cube and a short L-shaped
block. B, C and D do not have these blocks, so the answer is A.)

PAGE 59 — 2D VIEWS OF 3D SHAPES

Practice Questions

1.   A

There should be four blocks visible from
above, which rules out B, C and D.

(You can also find the answer to this question by looking at
the positions of the blocks — there should be two blocks on
the left of the figure, which rules out C and D. There should be
two blocks along the back of the figure, which rules out B.)

2.   D

There should be two blocks at the front of
the figure, which rules out A, B and C.

(You could start this question by counting the number of
blocks visible from above. There are four, which rules out
A. But then you would also have to look at the positions of
the blocks to work out whether the answer is B, C or D.)

3.   B

There should be six blocks visible from above, which rules out
C and D. There should be two blocks on the left-hand side
of the figure, which rules out A. The answer must be B.

(Questions where some blocks are floating can be tricky. The
stack of two floating blocks on the right of the figure touches the
row of blocks at the bottom. This tells you that if they were on
the ground, the cubes would be next to each other and the answer
should have a row of three squares at the front of the figure.)

PAGE 61 — CUBES AND NETS

Practice Questions

1.   D

The grey ellipse and the grey triangle should be on opposite
sides, which rules out A. There is no face with just two
white lines, so this rules out B. There is no face with a
white ellipse, which rules out C, so D is the answer.

2.   A

There is no face on the net with just two circles,
which rules out B. The letter 'A' and the grey triangle
should be on opposite sides, which rules out C. The
black triangle does not point to the cross-hatched
parallelogram on the net, which rules out D.

3.   C

The grey pentagon and the black ellipse should be
on opposite sides, which rules out A. The longest
lengths of the black ellipse and the hatched rectangle
should be parallel to each other, which rules out B. The
five-pointed star and the eleven-pointed star should be
on opposite sides, which rules out D, so C is the answer.

Index